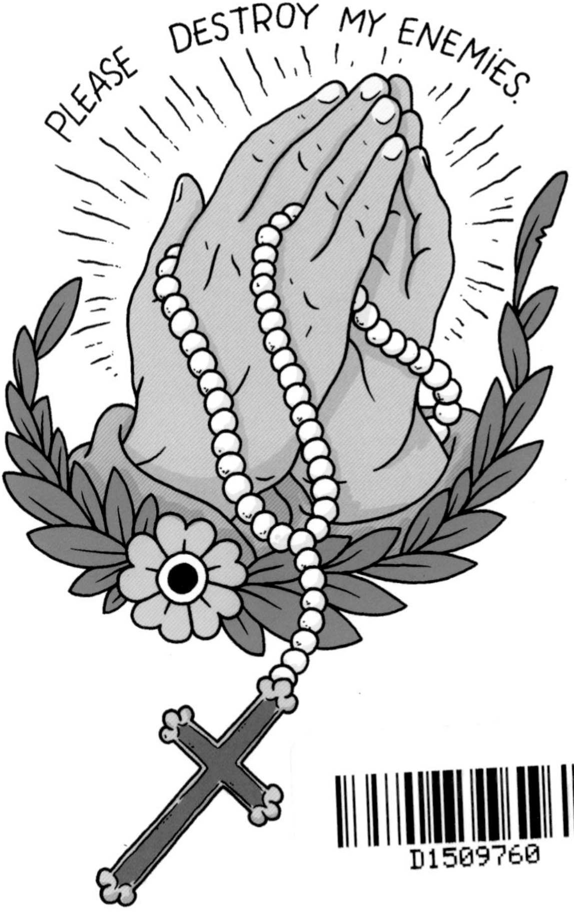
PLEASE DESTROY MY ENEMIES.

FOR RACHEL DUKES.

PUBLISHED BY SILVER SPROCKET
1057 VALENCIA STREET,
SAN FRANCISCO, CA 94110

WWW.SILVERSPROCKET.NET

ISBN 978-1-945509-21-6
PRINTED IN CANADA

SECOND PRINTING, 2018. NOW IN FULL COLOR!

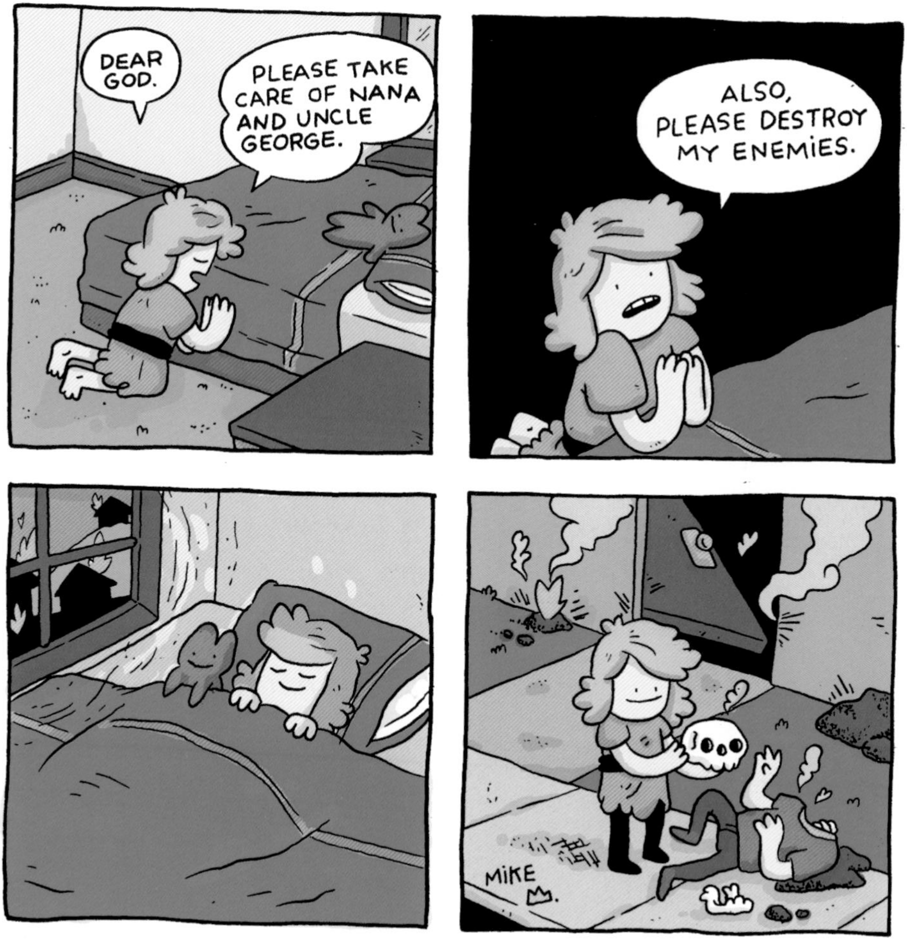
DEAR GOD.
PLEASE TAKE CARE OF NANA AND UNCLE GEORGE.
ALSO, PLEASE DESTROY MY ENEMIES.
MIKE

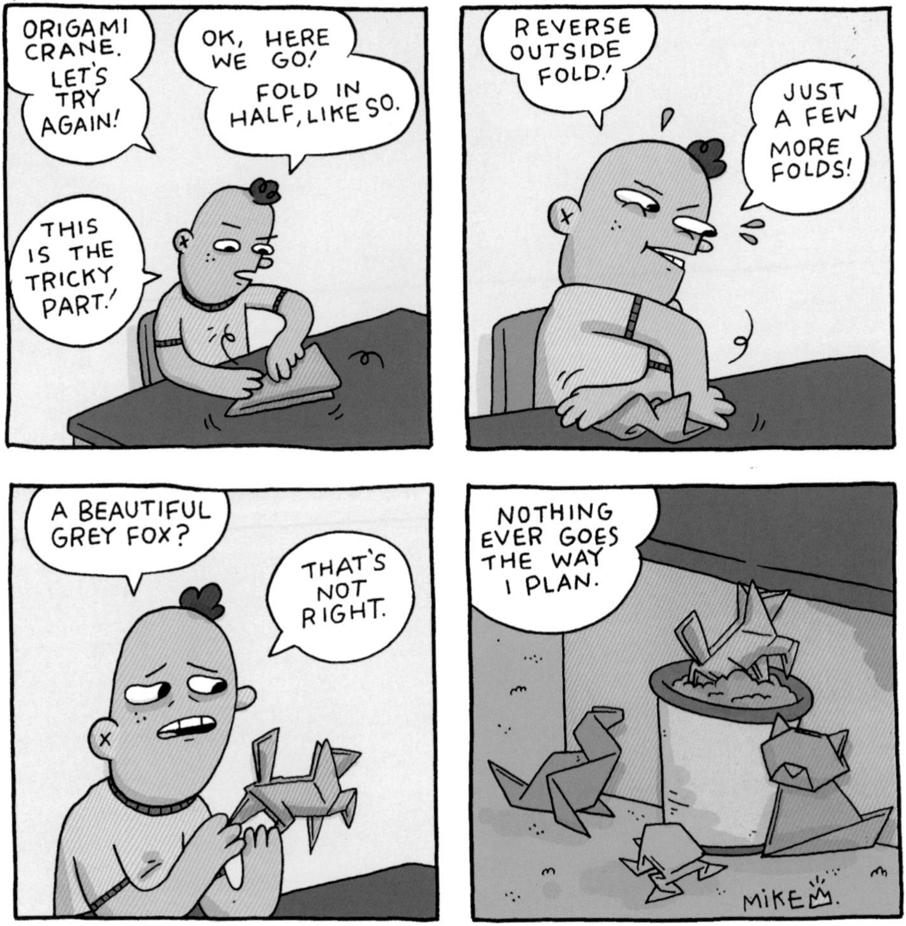
ORIGAMI CRANE. LET'S TRY AGAIN!
OK, HERE WE GO!
FOLD IN HALF, LIKE SO.
THIS IS THE TRICKY PART!
REVERSE OUTSIDE FOLD!
JUST A FEW MORE FOLDS!
A BEAUTIFUL GREY FOX?
THAT'S NOT RIGHT.
NOTHING EVER GOES THE WAY I PLAN.
MIKE

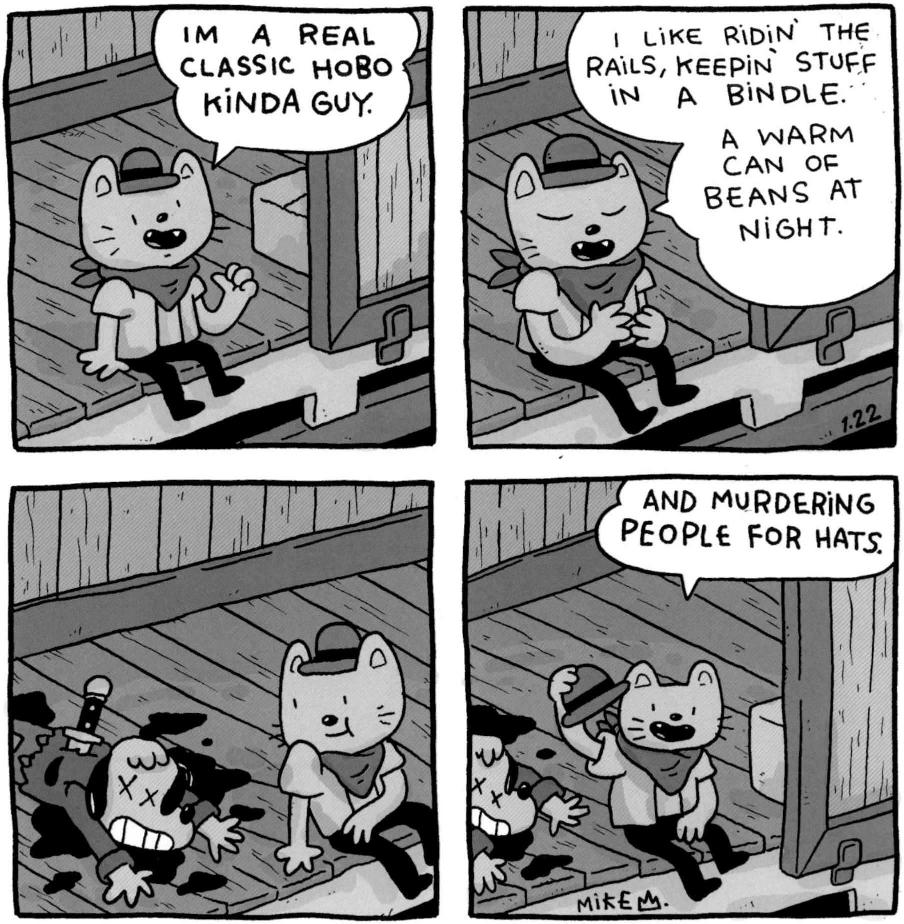
IM A REAL CLASSIC HOBO KINDA GUY.
I LIKE RIDIN' THE RAILS, KEEPIN' STUFF IN A BINDLE.
A WARM CAN OF BEANS AT NIGHT.
1.22
AND MURDERING PEOPLE FOR HATS.
MIKE M.

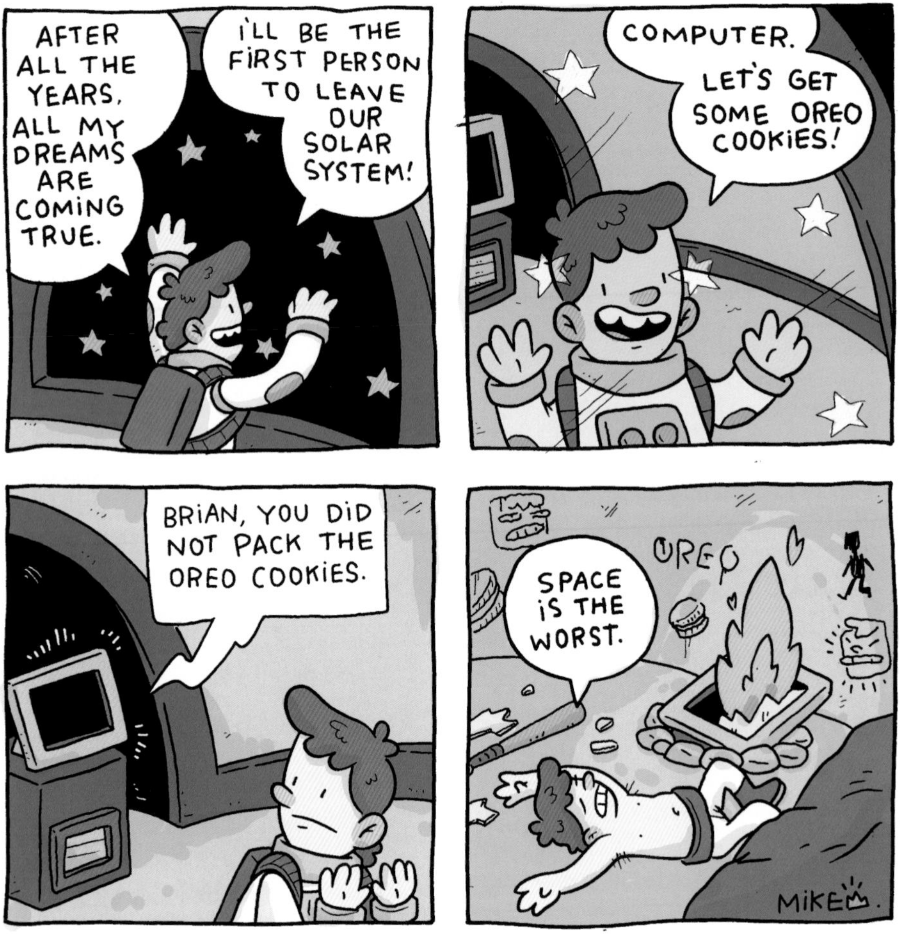
AFTER ALL THE YEARS, ALL MY DREAMS ARE COMING TRUE.
I'LL BE THE FIRST PERSON TO LEAVE OUR SOLAR SYSTEM!
COMPUTER.
LET'S GET SOME OREO COOKIES!
BRIAN, YOU DID NOT PACK THE OREO COOKIES.
OREO
SPACE IS THE WORST.
MIKE

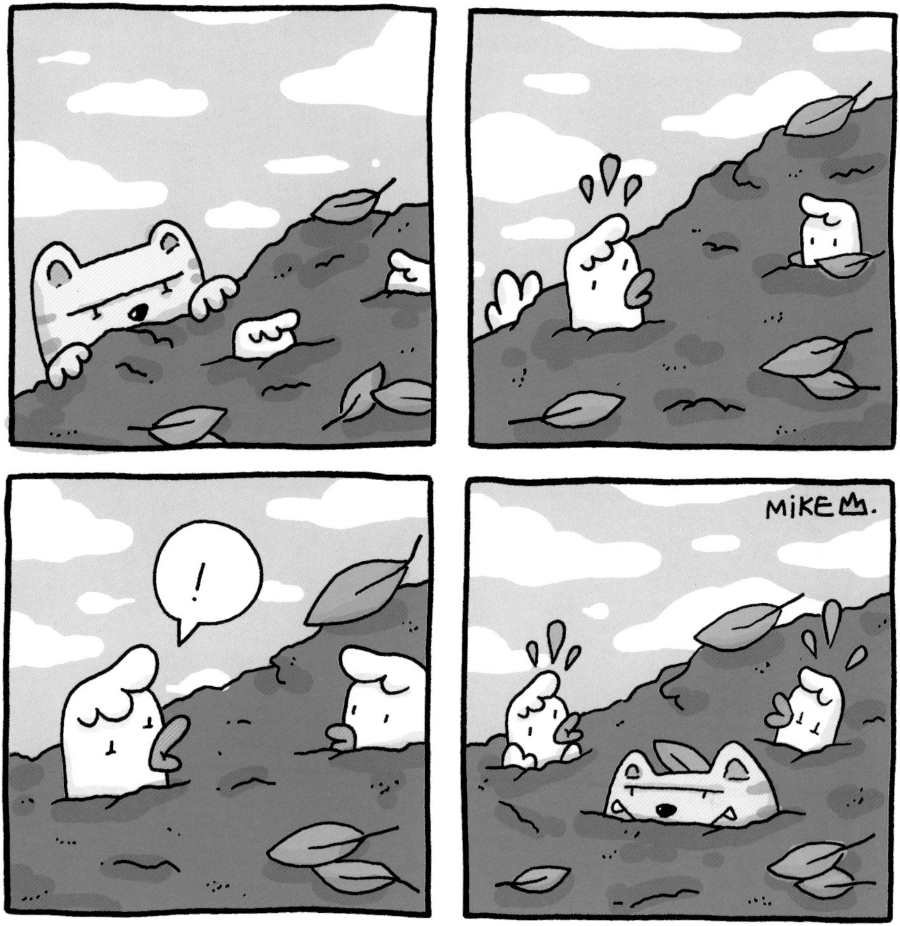
!
MIKE M.

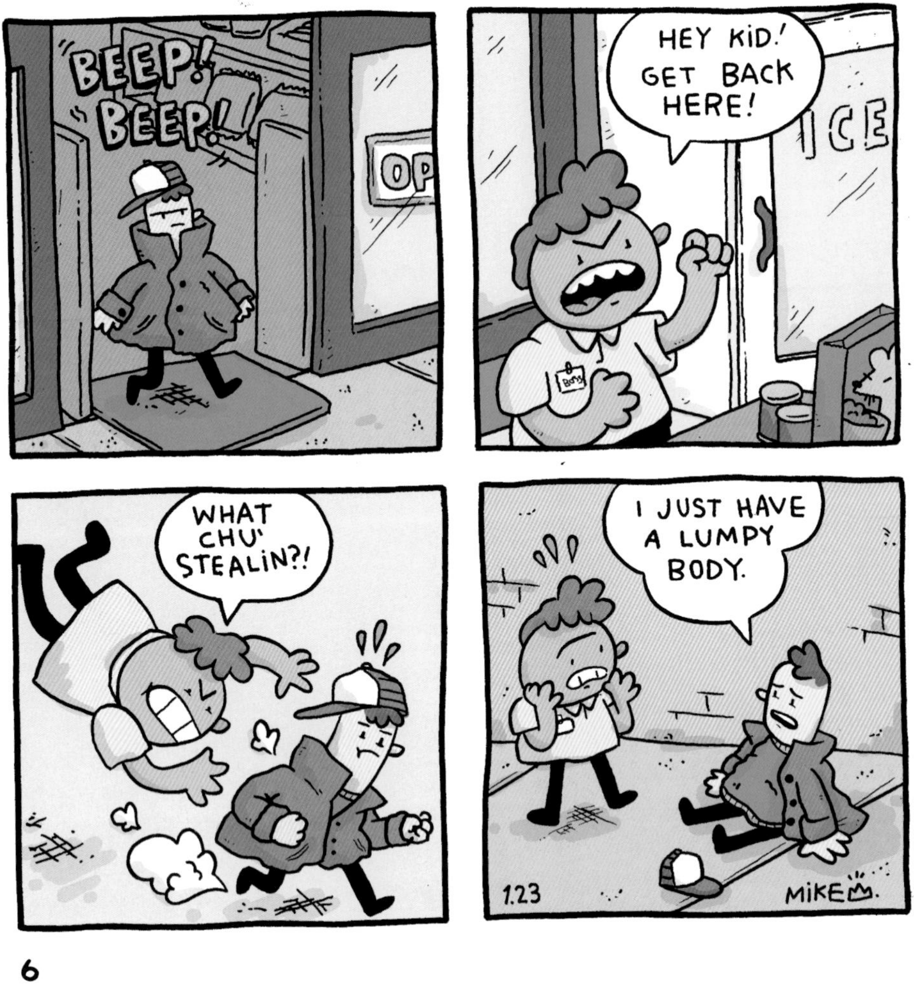
BEEP! BEEP!
OP
HEY KID! GET BACK HERE!
ICE
BOSS
WHAT CHU' STEALIN?!
I JUST HAVE A LUMPY BODY.
1.23
MIKE

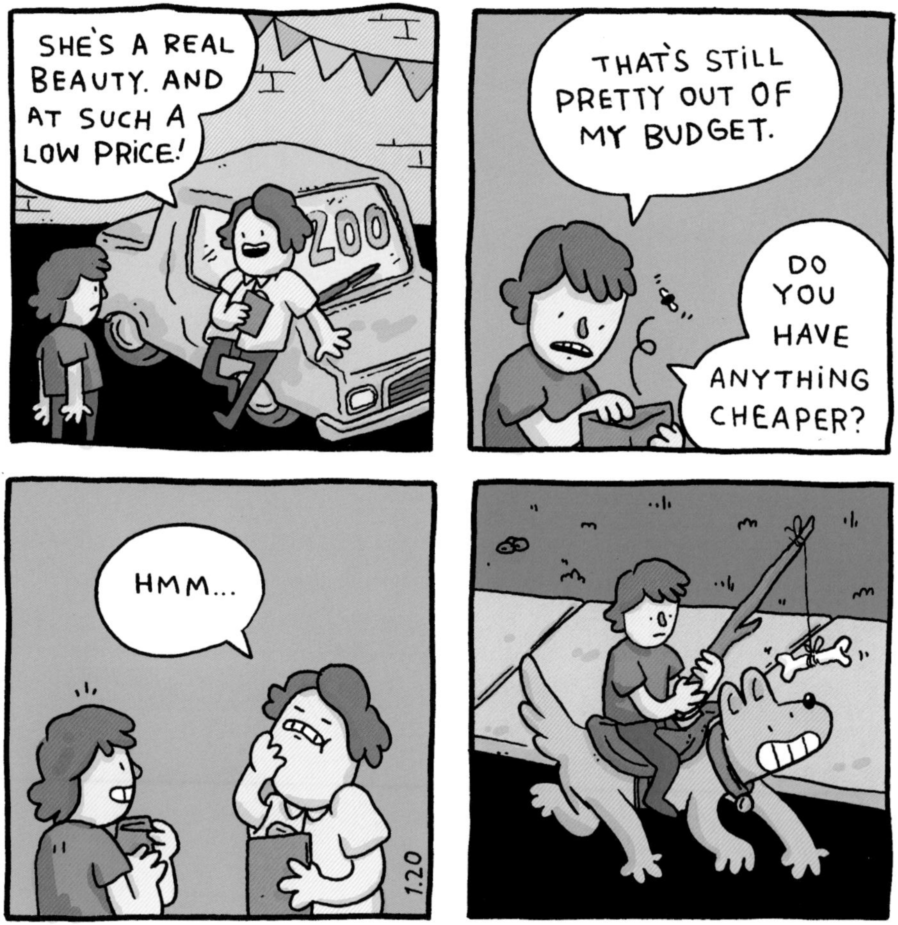
SHE'S A REAL BEAUTY. AND AT SUCH A LOW PRICE!
$200
THAT'S STILL PRETTY OUT OF MY BUDGET.
DO YOU HAVE ANYTHING CHEAPER?
HMM...
1.20

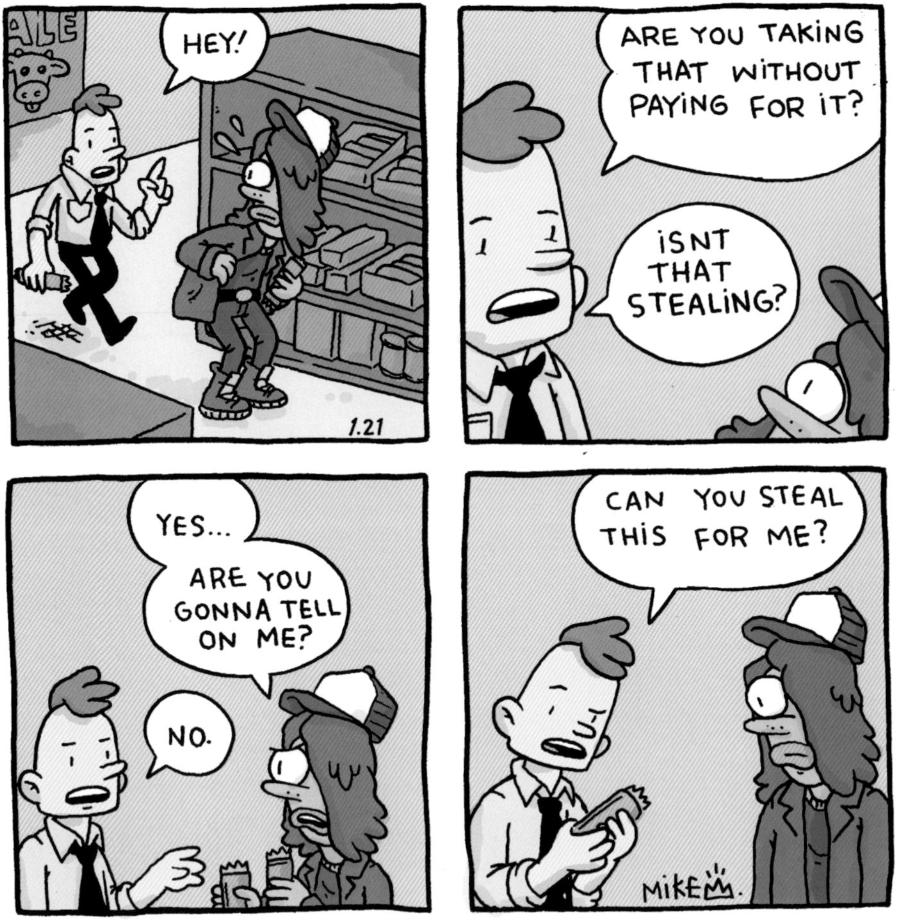
ALE
HEY!
1.21
ARE YOU TAKING THAT WITHOUT PAYING FOR IT?
ISNT THAT STEALING?
YES...
ARE YOU GONNA TELL ON ME?
NO.
CAN YOU STEAL THIS FOR ME?
MIKE

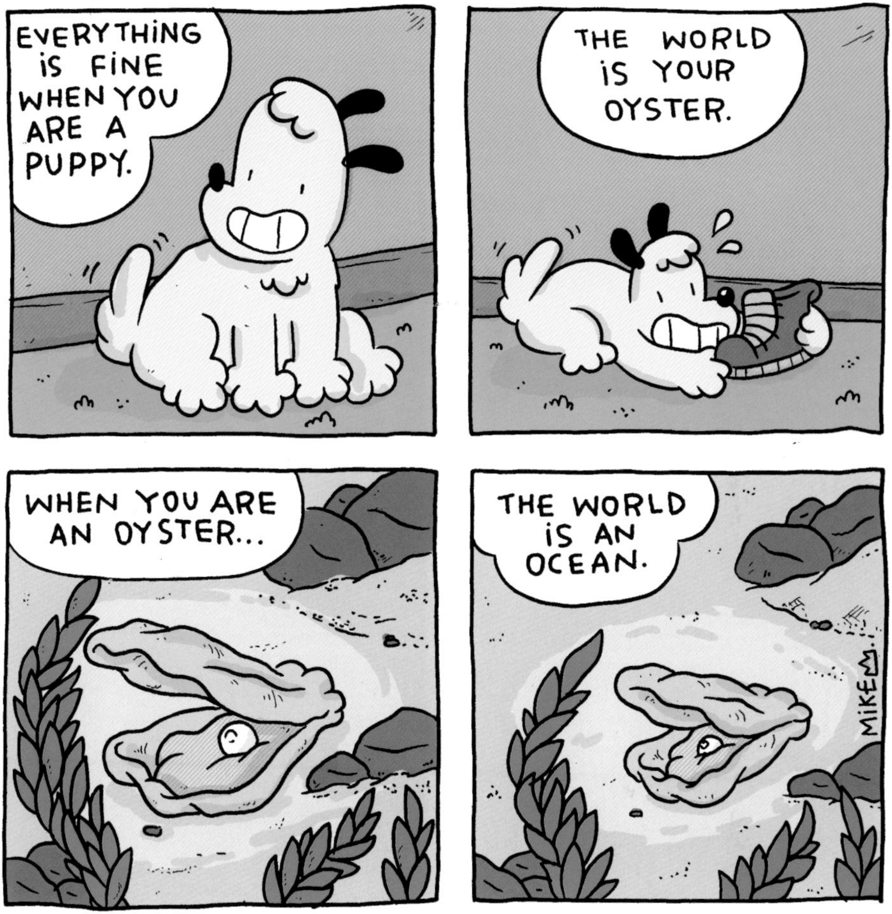
EVERYTHING IS FINE WHEN YOU ARE A PUPPY.
THE WORLD IS YOUR OYSTER.
WHEN YOU ARE AN OYSTER...
THE WORLD IS AN OCEAN.
MIKE

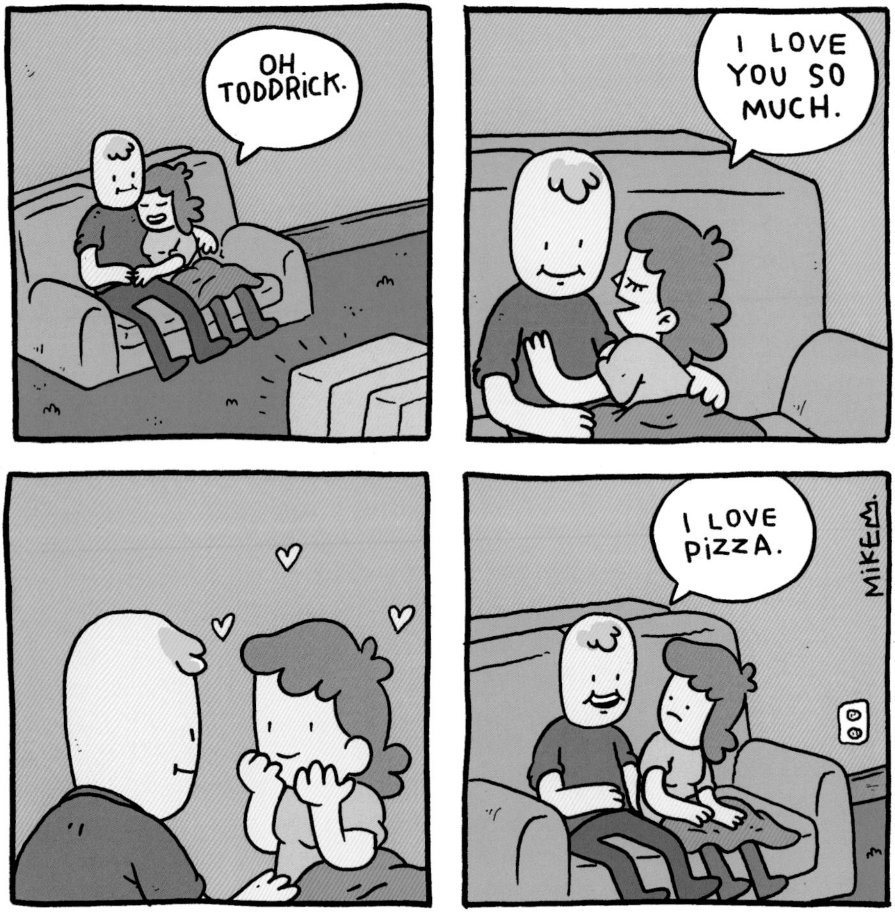
OH TODDRICK.
I LOVE YOU SO MUCH.
I LOVE PIZZA.
MIKEM.

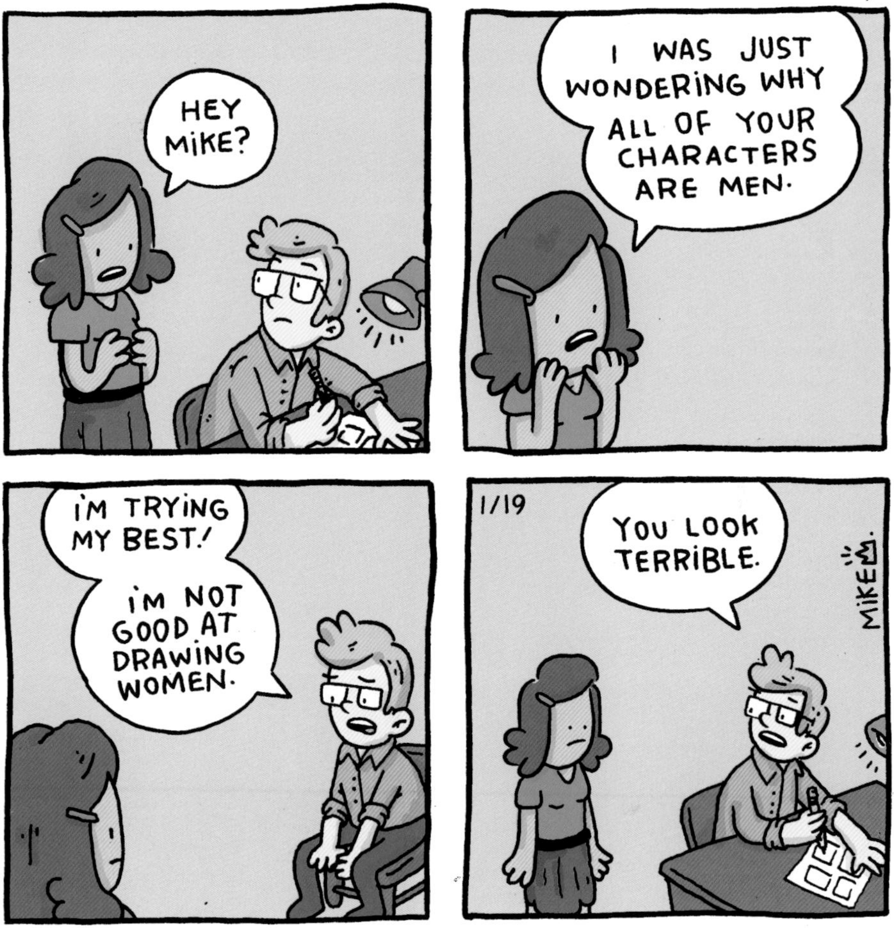
HEY MIKE?
I WAS JUST WONDERING WHY ALL OF YOUR CHARACTERS ARE MEN.
I'M TRYING MY BEST!
I'M NOT GOOD AT DRAWING WOMEN.
1/19
YOU LOOK TERRIBLE.
MIKE

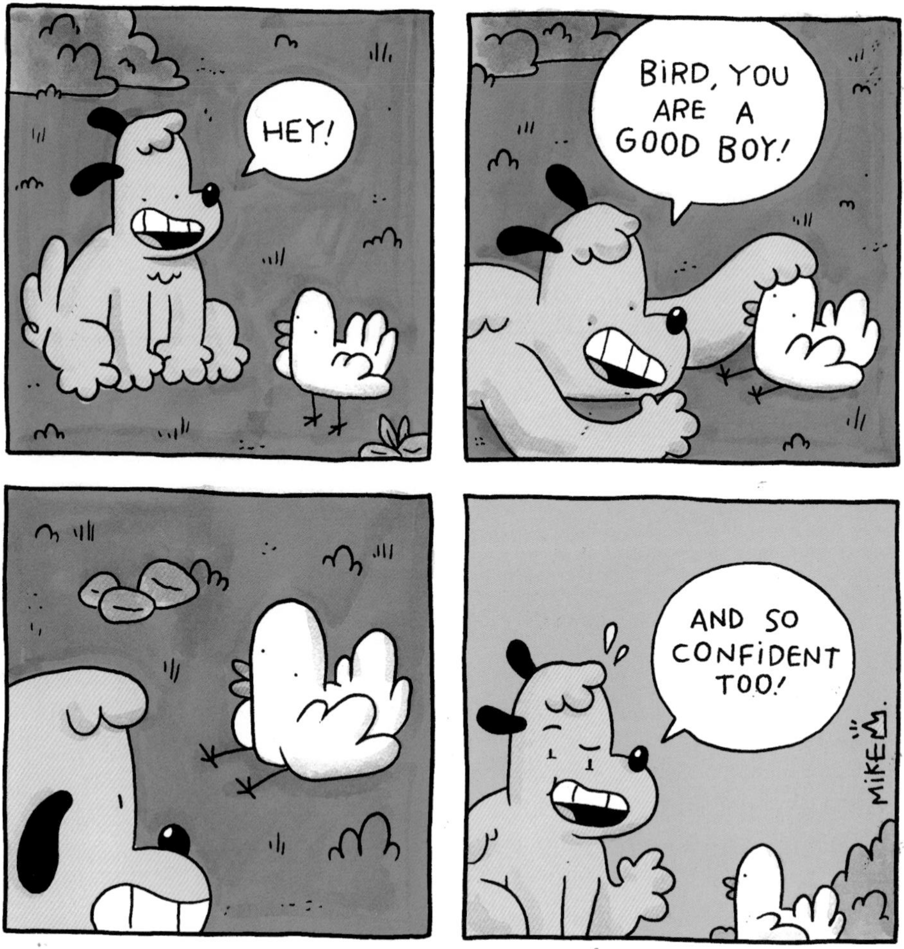
HEY!
BIRD, YOU ARE A GOOD BOY!
AND SO CONFIDENT TOO!
MIKE M.

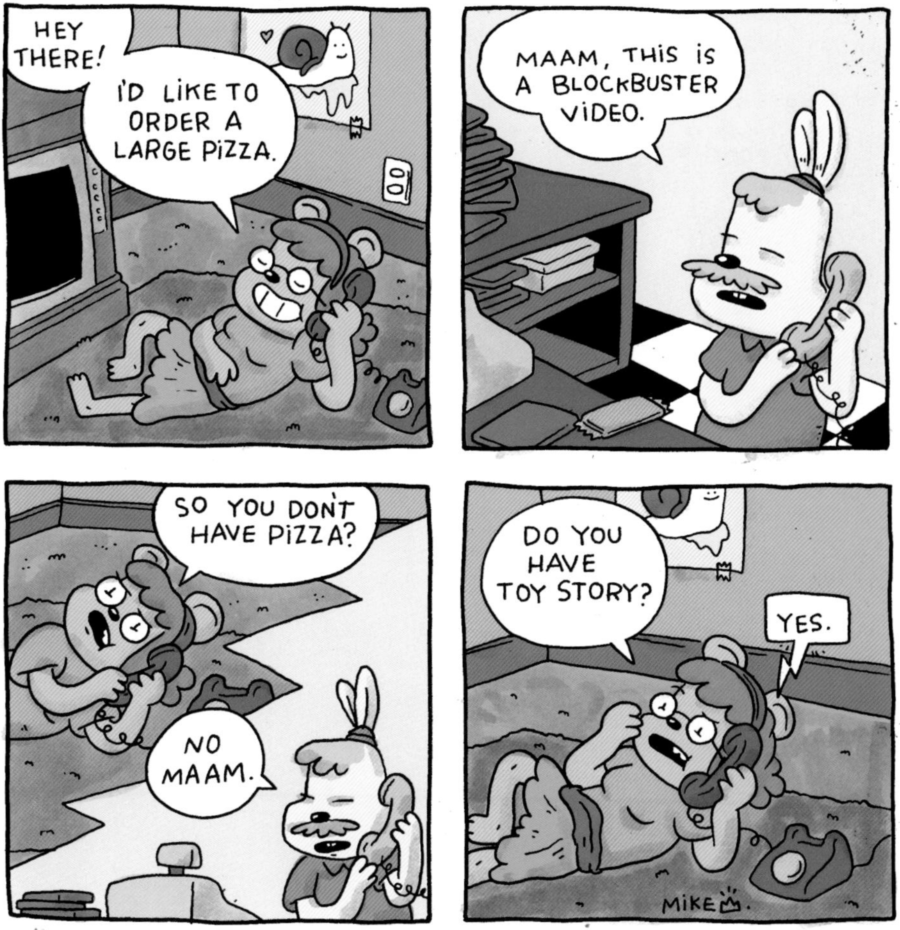
HEY THERE!
I'D LIKE TO ORDER A LARGE PIZZA.
MAAM, THIS IS A BLOCKBUSTER VIDEO.
SO YOU DON'T HAVE PIZZA?
NO MAAM.
DO YOU HAVE TOY STORY?
YES.
MIKE

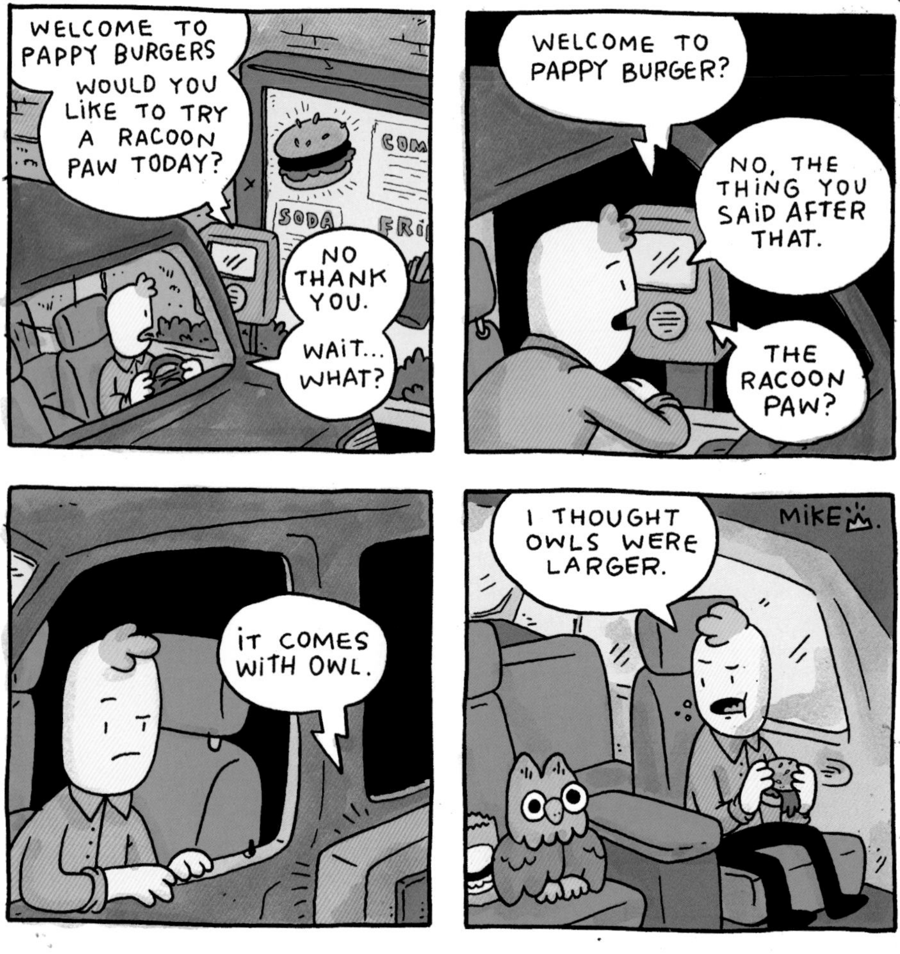
WELCOME TO PAPPY BURGERS
WOULD YOU LIKE TO TRY A RACOON PAW TODAY?
SODA
NO THANK YOU.
WAIT... WHAT?
WELCOME TO PAPPY BURGER?
NO, THE THING YOU SAID AFTER THAT.
THE RACOON PAW?
IT COMES WITH OWL.
I THOUGHT OWLS WERE LARGER.
MIKE.

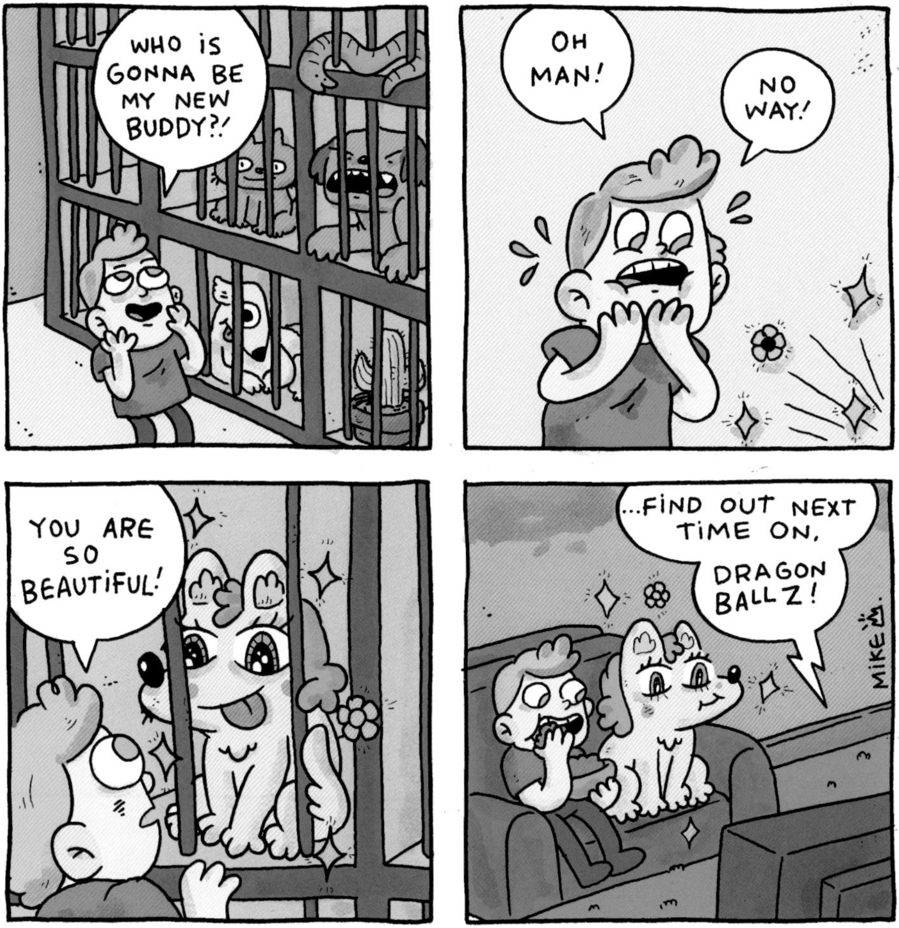
WHO IS GONNA BE MY NEW BUDDY?!
OH MAN!
NO WAY!
YOU ARE SO BEAUTIFUL!
...FIND OUT NEXT TIME ON, DRAGON BALL Z!
MIKE

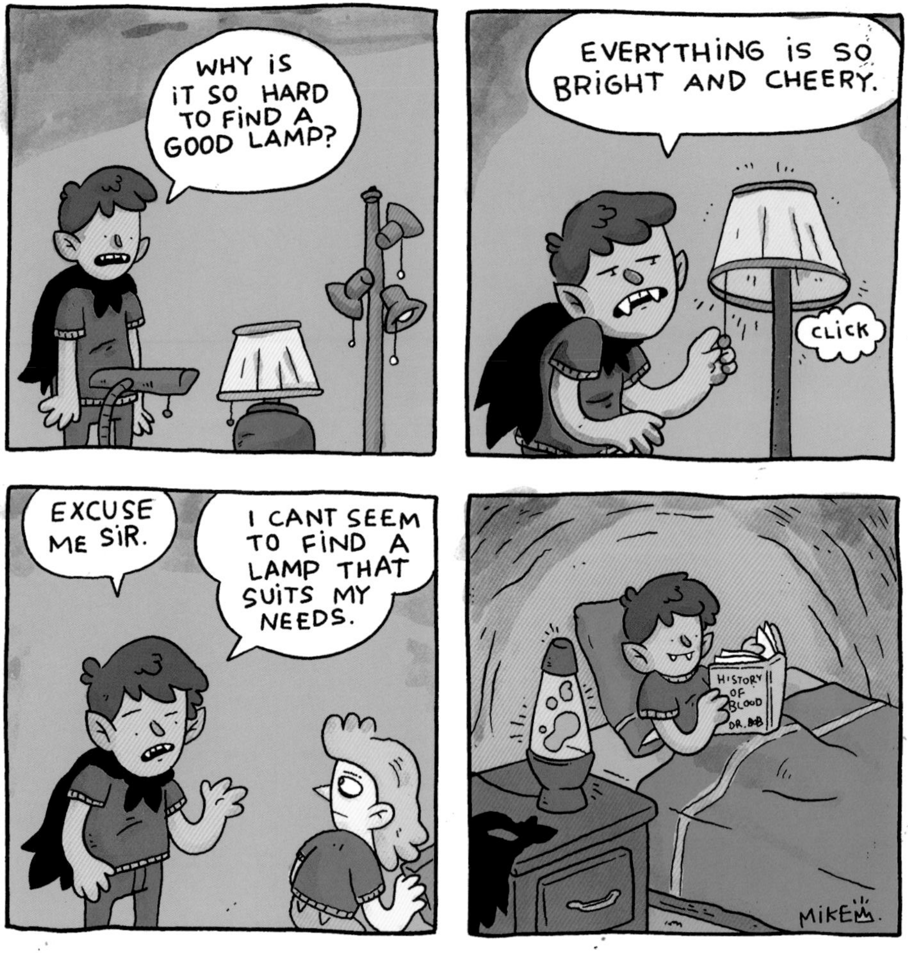
WHY IS IT SO HARD TO FIND A GOOD LAMP?
EVERYTHING IS SO BRIGHT AND CHEERY.
CLICK
EXCUSE ME SIR.
I CANT SEEM TO FIND A LAMP THAT SUITS MY NEEDS.
HISTORY OF BLOOD
MIKE

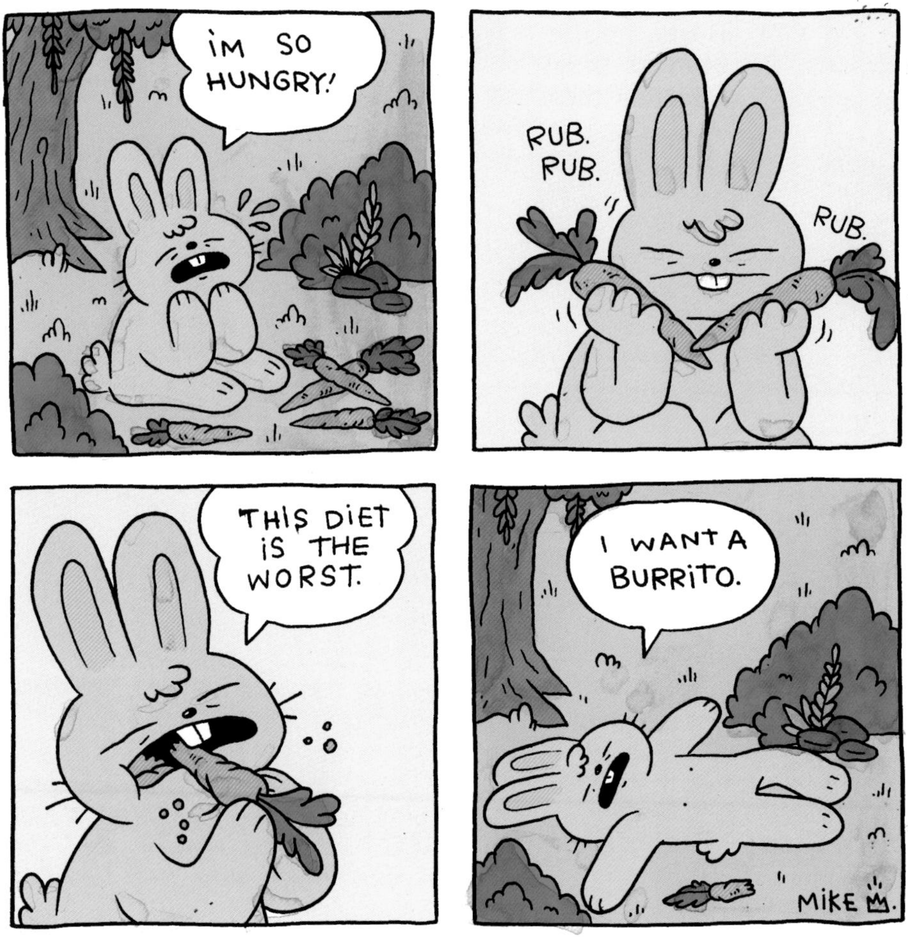
IM SO HUNGRY!
RUB. RUB.
RUB.
THIS DIET IS THE WORST.
I WANT A BURRITO.
MIKE

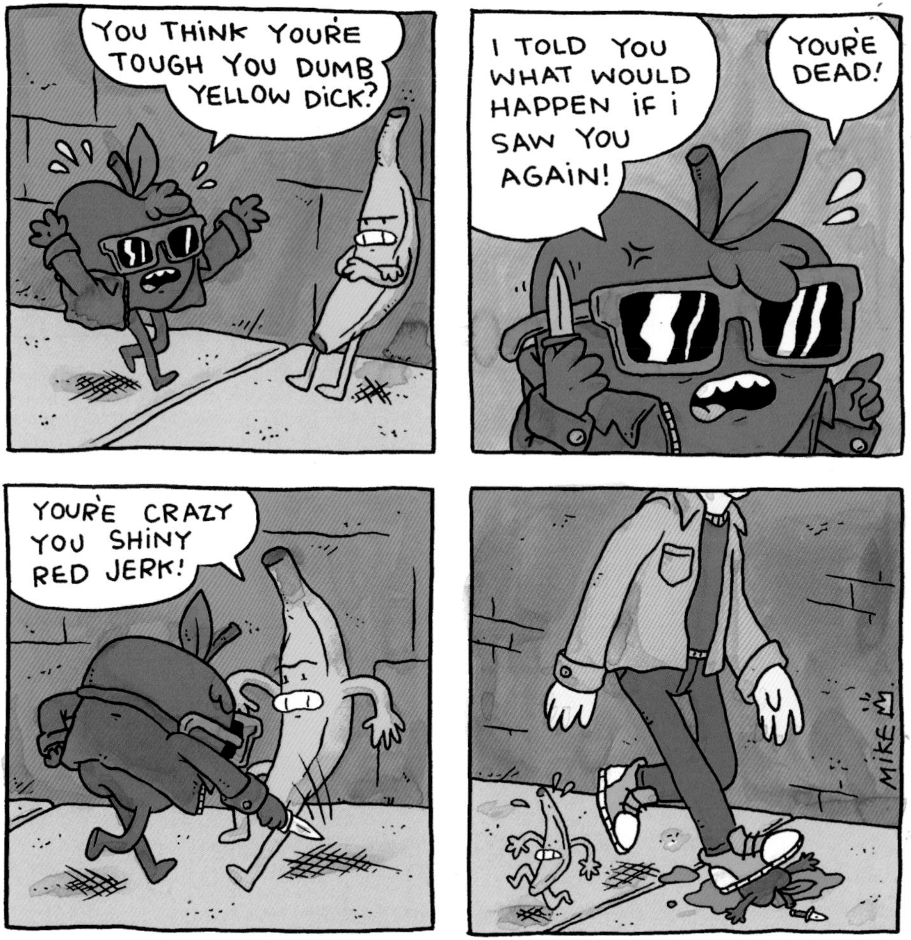
YOU THINK YOU'RE TOUGH YOU DUMB YELLOW DICK?
I TOLD YOU WHAT WOULD HAPPEN IF I SAW YOU AGAIN!
YOU'RE DEAD!
YOU'RE CRAZY YOU SHINY RED JERK!
MIKE M.

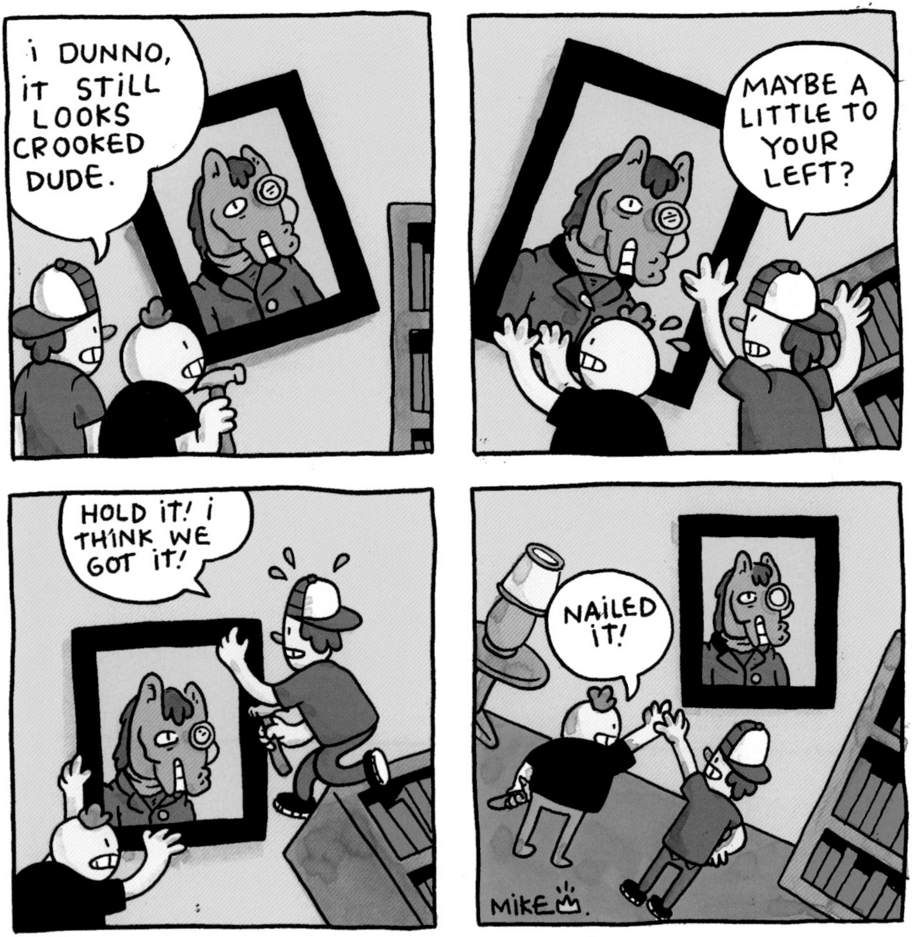
i DUNNO, iT STiLL LOOKS CROOKED DUDE.
MAYBE A LITTLE TO YOUR LEFT?
HOLD iT! i THiNK WE GOT iT!
NAiLED iT!
MiKE

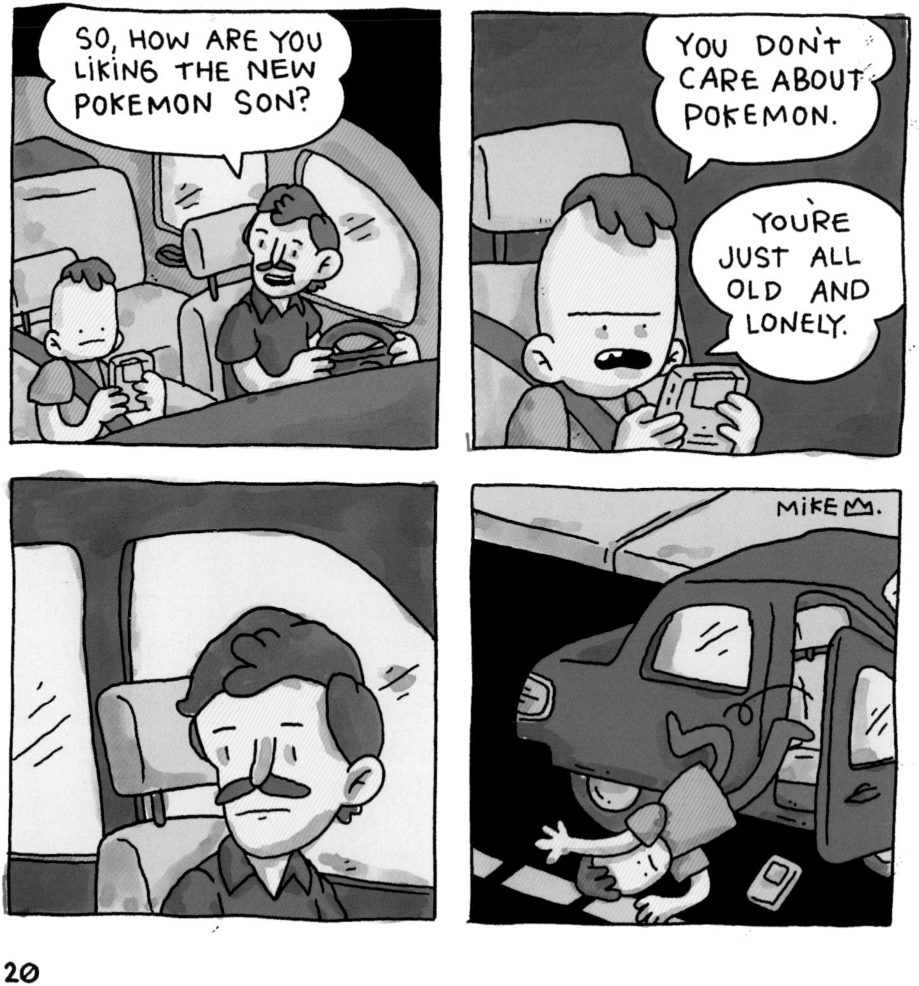
SO, HOW ARE YOU LIKING THE NEW POKEMON SON?
YOU DON'T CARE ABOUT POKEMON.
YOU'RE JUST ALL OLD AND LONELY.
MIKE M.

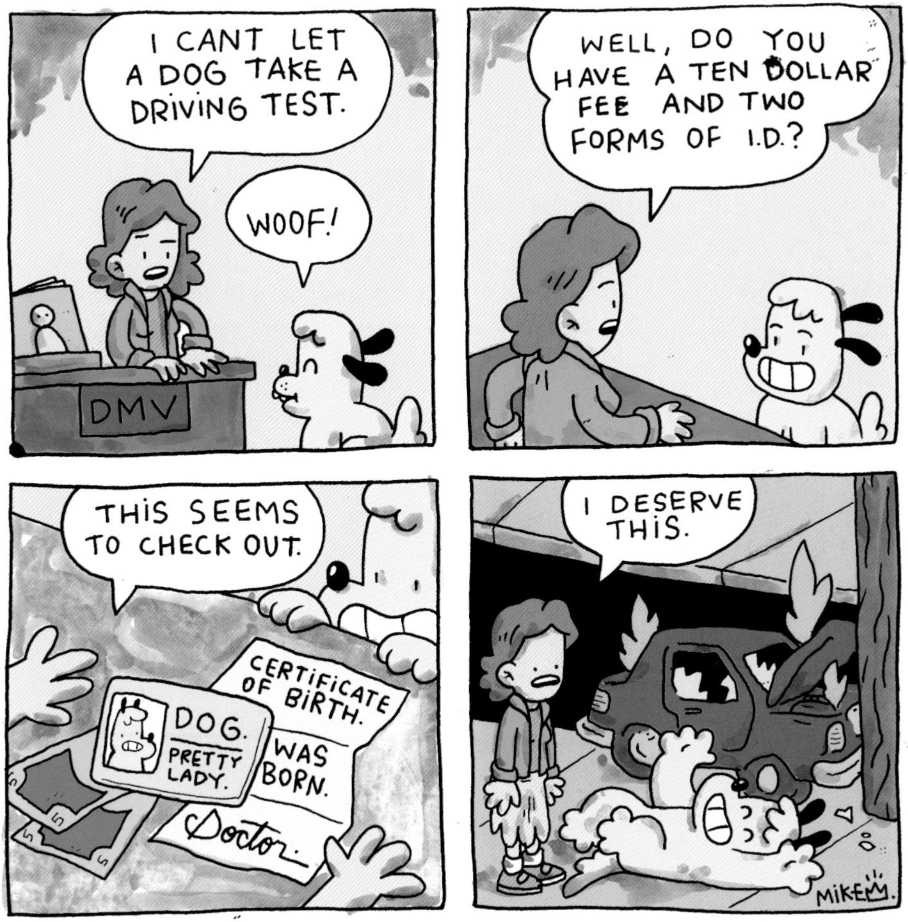
I CANT LET A DOG TAKE A DRIVING TEST.
WOOF!
DMV
WELL, DO YOU HAVE A TEN DOLLAR FEE AND TWO FORMS OF I.D.?
THIS SEEMS TO CHECK OUT.
DOG. PRETTY LADY.
CERTIFICATE OF BIRTH.
WAS BORN.
Doctor.
I DESERVE THIS.
MIKE

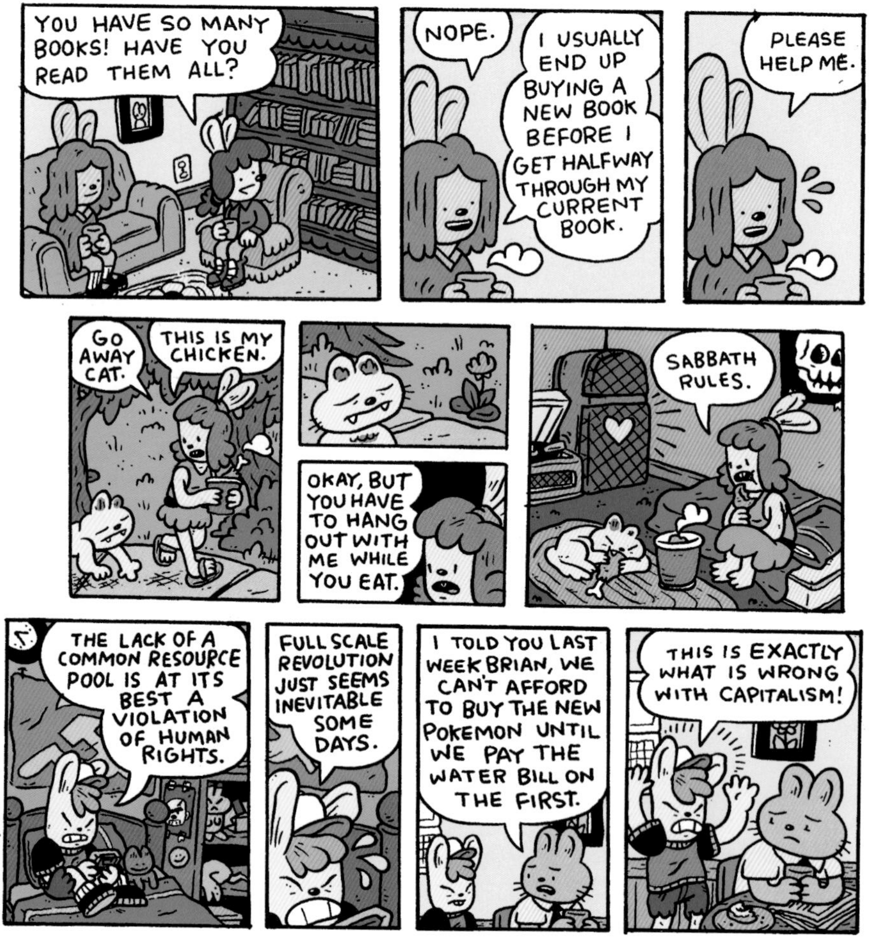
YOU HAVE SO MANY BOOKS! HAVE YOU READ THEM ALL?
NOPE.
I USUALLY END UP BUYING A NEW BOOK BEFORE I GET HALFWAY THROUGH MY CURRENT BOOK.
PLEASE HELP ME.
GO AWAY CAT.
THIS IS MY CHICKEN.
OKAY, BUT YOU HAVE TO HANG OUT WITH ME WHILE YOU EAT.
SABBATH RULES.
THE LACK OF A COMMON RESOURCE POOL IS AT ITS BEST A VIOLATION OF HUMAN RIGHTS.
FULL SCALE REVOLUTION JUST SEEMS INEVITABLE SOME DAYS.
I TOLD YOU LAST WEEK BRIAN, WE CAN'T AFFORD TO BUY THE NEW POKEMON UNTIL WE PAY THE WATER BILL ON THE FIRST.
THIS IS EXACTLY WHAT IS WRONG WITH CAPITALISM!

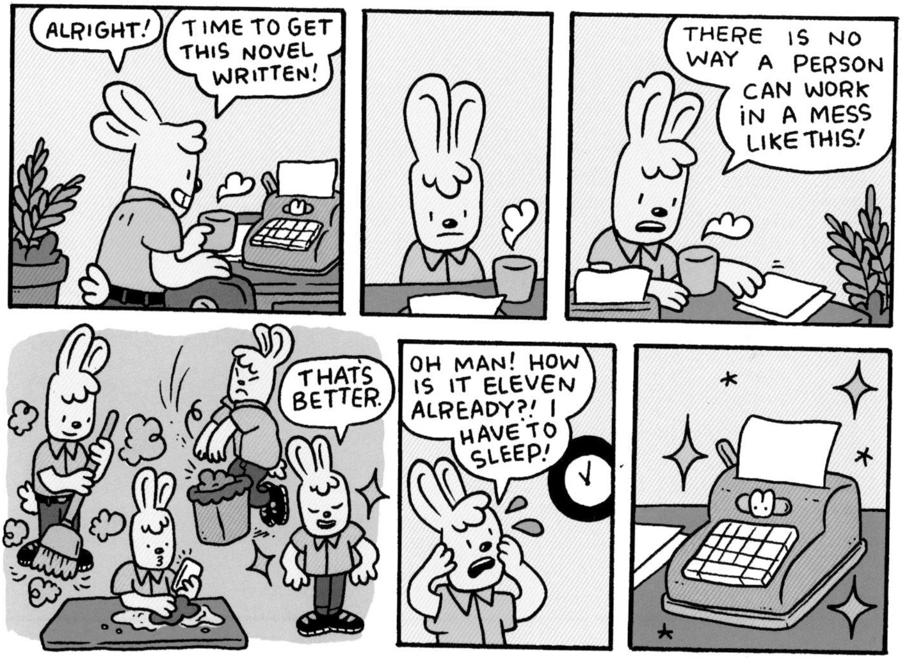
ALRIGHT!
TIME TO GET THIS NOVEL WRITTEN!
THERE IS NO WAY A PERSON CAN WORK IN A MESS LIKE THIS!
THAT'S BETTER.
OH MAN! HOW IS IT ELEVEN ALREADY?! I HAVE TO SLEEP!

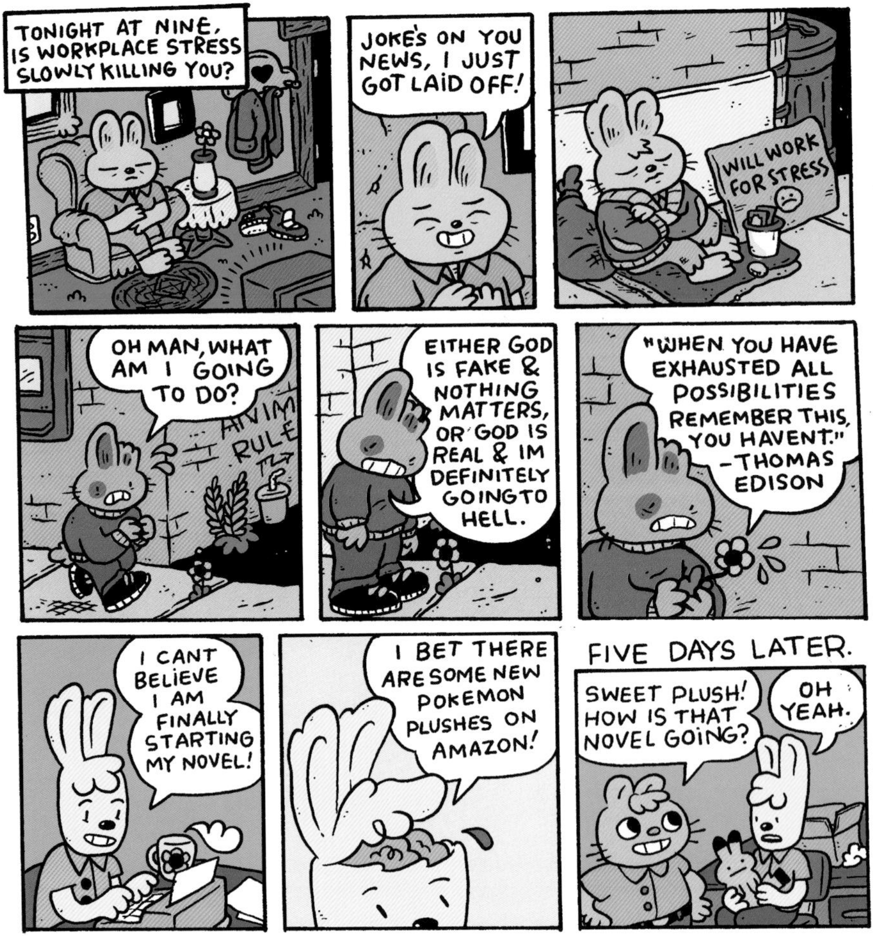
TONIGHT AT NINE, IS WORKPLACE STRESS SLOWLY KILLING YOU?
JOKE'S ON YOU NEWS, I JUST GOT LAID OFF!
WILL WORK FOR STRESS
OH MAN, WHAT AM I GOING TO DO?
EITHER GOD IS FAKE & NOTHING MATTERS, OR GOD IS REAL & IM DEFINITELY GOING TO HELL.
"WHEN YOU HAVE EXHAUSTED ALL POSSIBILITIES REMEMBER THIS, YOU HAVENT." -THOMAS EDISON
I CANT BELIEVE I AM FINALLY STARTING MY NOVEL!
I BET THERE ARE SOME NEW POKEMON PLUSHES ON AMAZON!
FIVE DAYS LATER.
SWEET PLUSH! HOW IS THAT NOVEL GOING?
OH YEAH.

AND THAT'S THE GIST OF THIS QUARTERLY REVIEW.
ANYTHING UNCLEAR?
I CANT FIGURE OUT WHY WE'RE ON THE ROOF.
OR DOING THIS ON CHRISTMAS.
IN THE SNOW.
IT'S AN ITALIAN MANAGEMENT STRATEGY.
I HEARD ABOUT IT ON A PODCAST.
I THINK THIS MEETING WENT WELL.

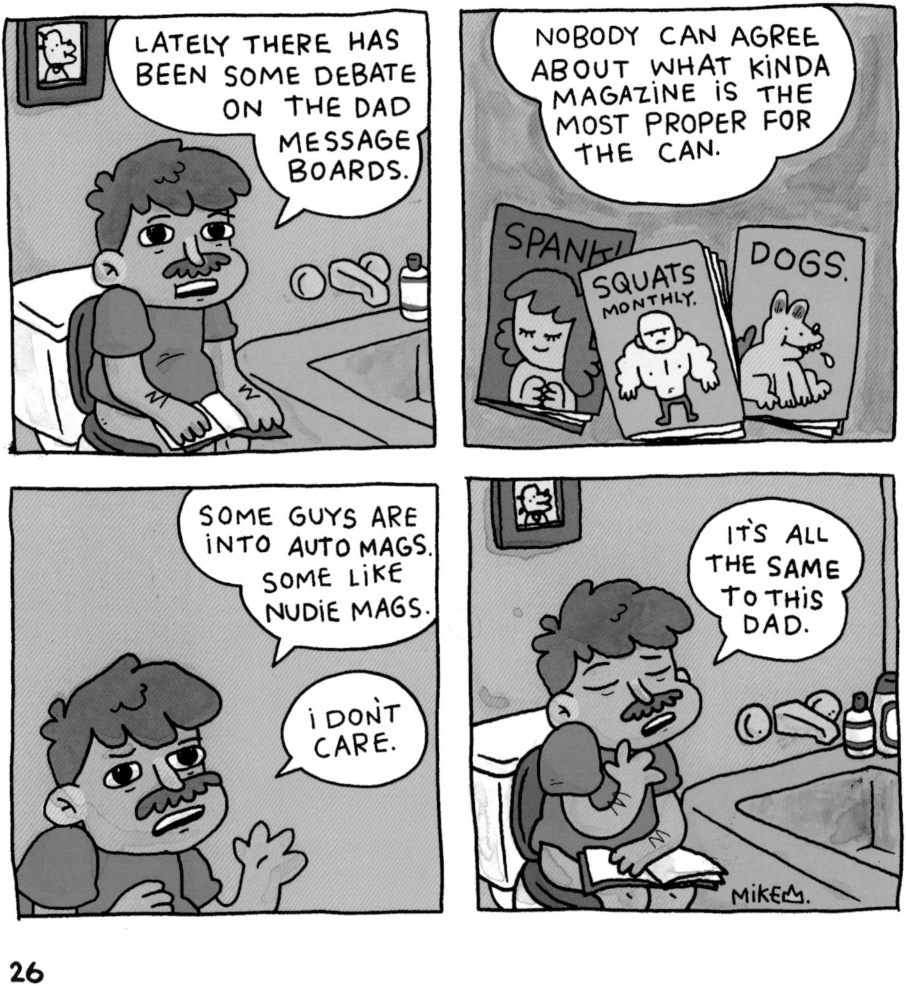
LATELY THERE HAS BEEN SOME DEBATE ON THE DAD MESSAGE BOARDS.
NOBODY CAN AGREE ABOUT WHAT KINDA MAGAZINE IS THE MOST PROPER FOR THE CAN.
SQUATS MONTHLY.
DOGS.
SOME GUYS ARE INTO AUTO MAGS. SOME LIKE NUDIE MAGS.
I DON'T CARE.
IT'S ALL THE SAME TO THIS DAD.
MIKE M.

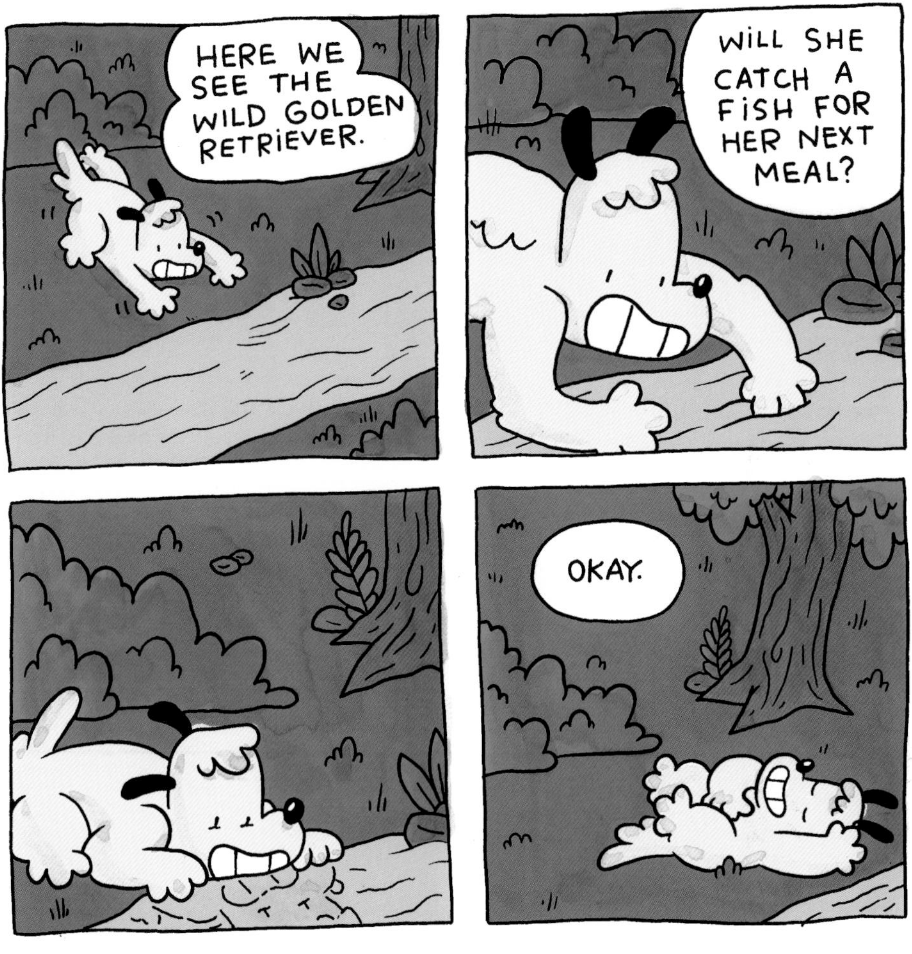
HERE WE SEE THE WILD GOLDEN RETRIEVER.
WILL SHE CATCH A FISH FOR HER NEXT MEAL?
OKAY.

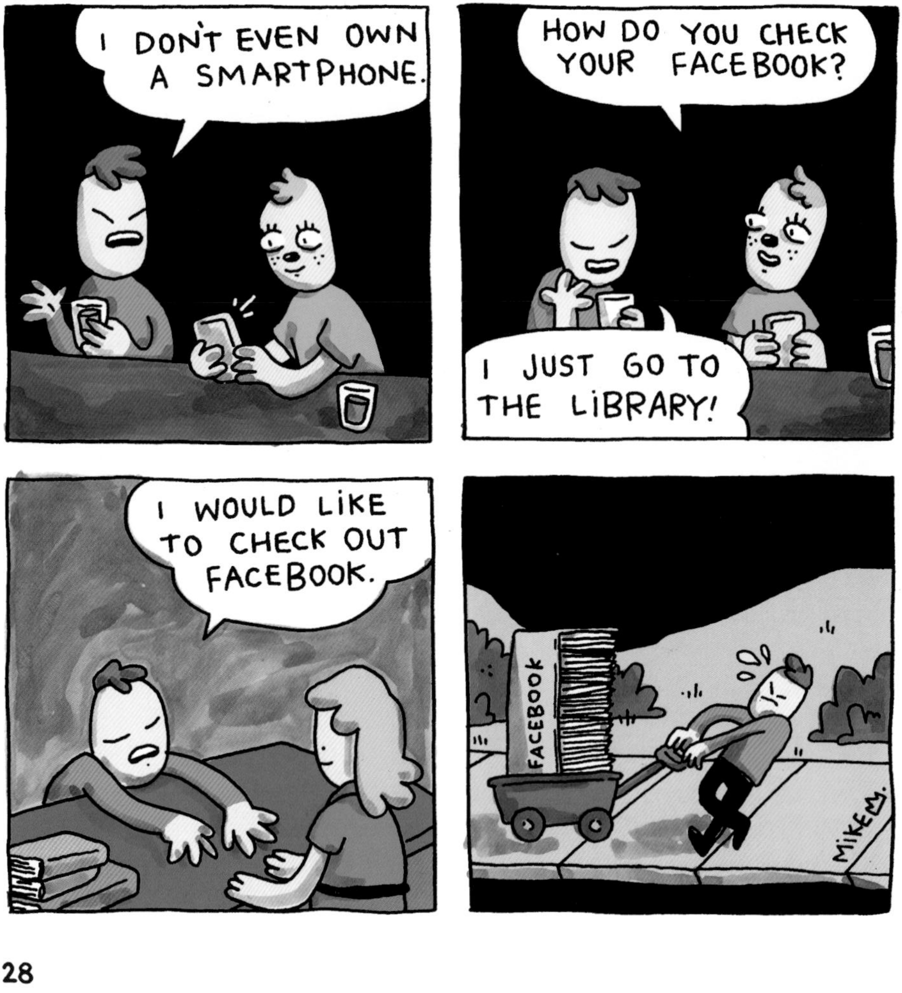
I DON'T EVEN OWN A SMARTPHONE.
HOW DO YOU CHECK YOUR FACEBOOK?
I JUST GO TO THE LIBRARY!
I WOULD LIKE TO CHECK OUT FACEBOOK.
FACEBOOK
MIKEM.

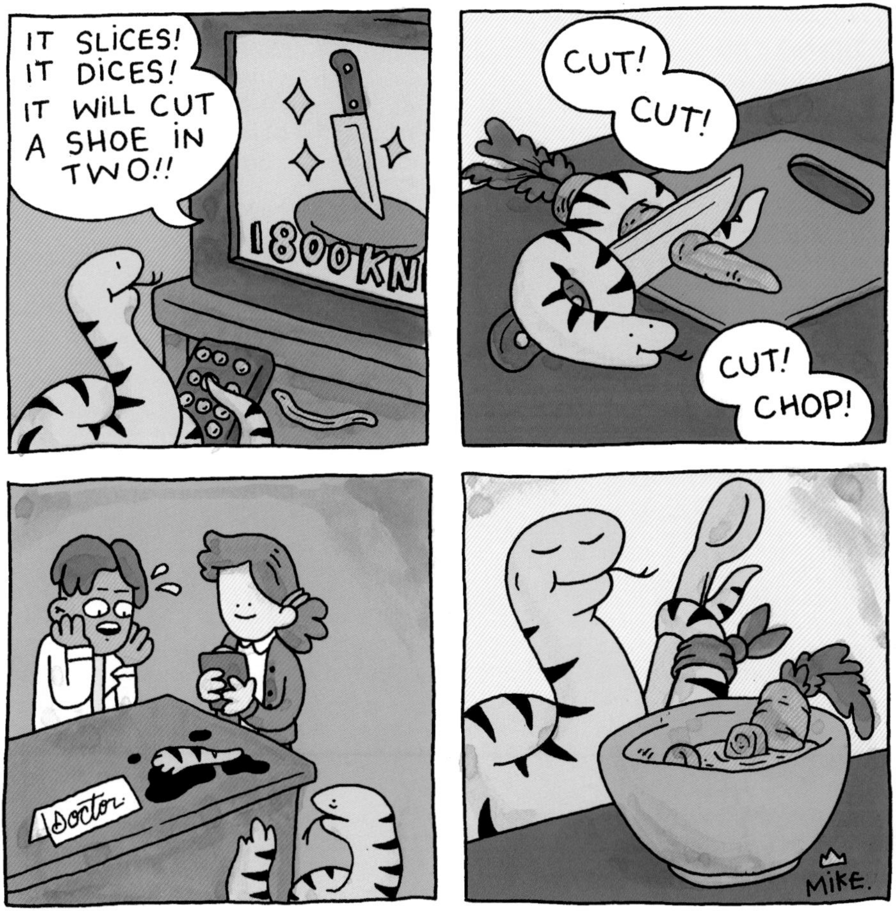
IT SLICES! IT DICES! IT WILL CUT A SHOE IN TWO!!
1800KN
CUT!
CUT!
CUT! CHOP!
Doctor
MIKE.

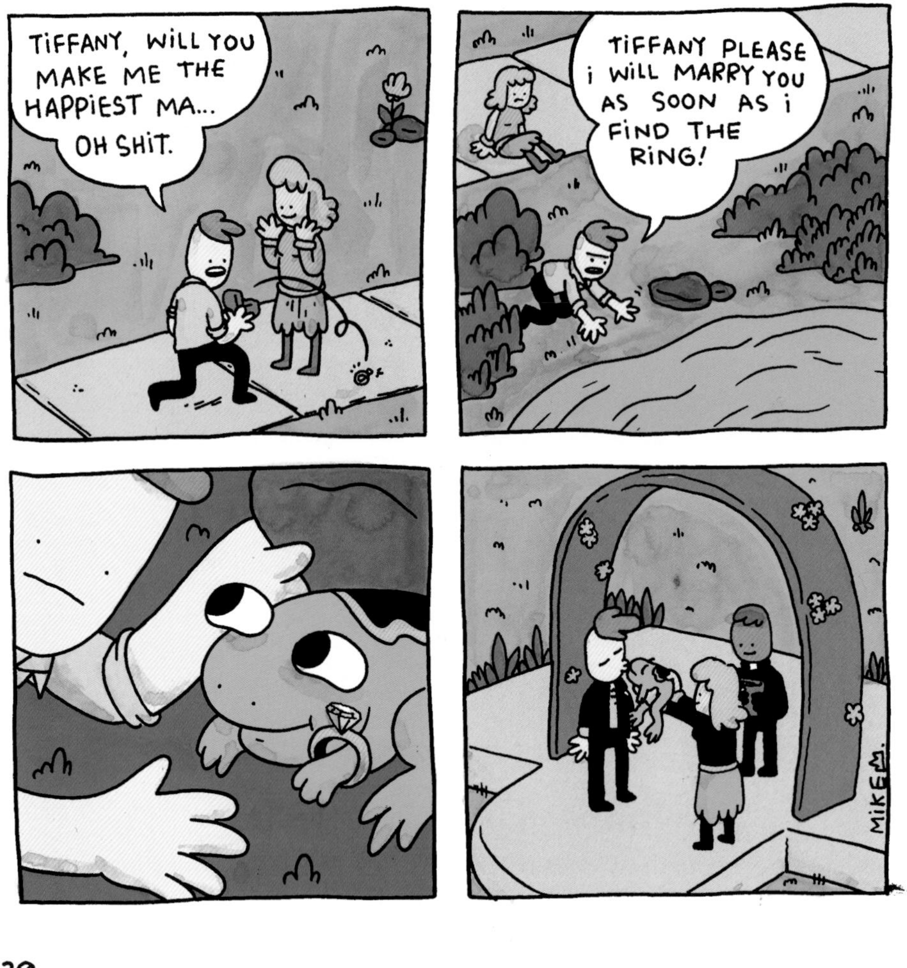
TIFFANY, WILL YOU MAKE ME THE HAPPIEST MA... OH SHIT.
TIFFANY PLEASE I WILL MARRY YOU AS SOON AS I FIND THE RING!
MIKE M.

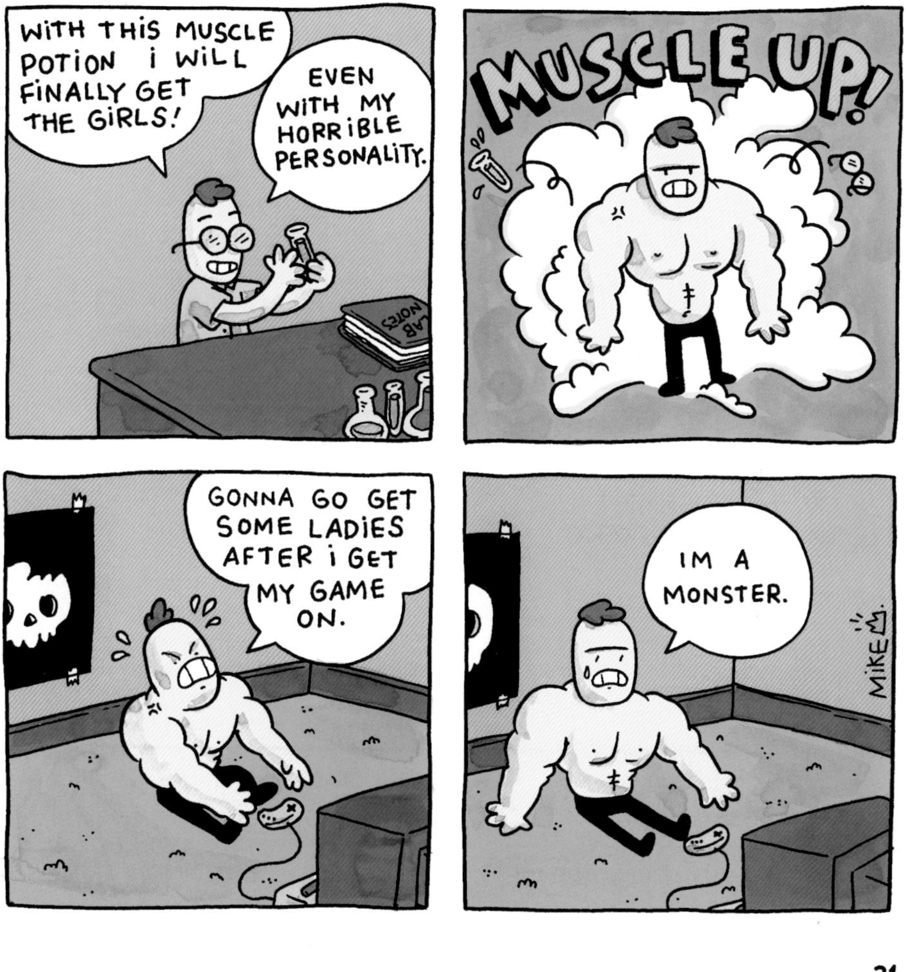
WITH THIS MUSCLE POTION I WILL FINALLY GET THE GIRLS!
EVEN WITH MY HORRIBLE PERSONALITY.
LAB NOTES
MUSCLE UP!
GONNA GO GET SOME LADIES AFTER I GET MY GAME ON.
IM A MONSTER.
MIKE

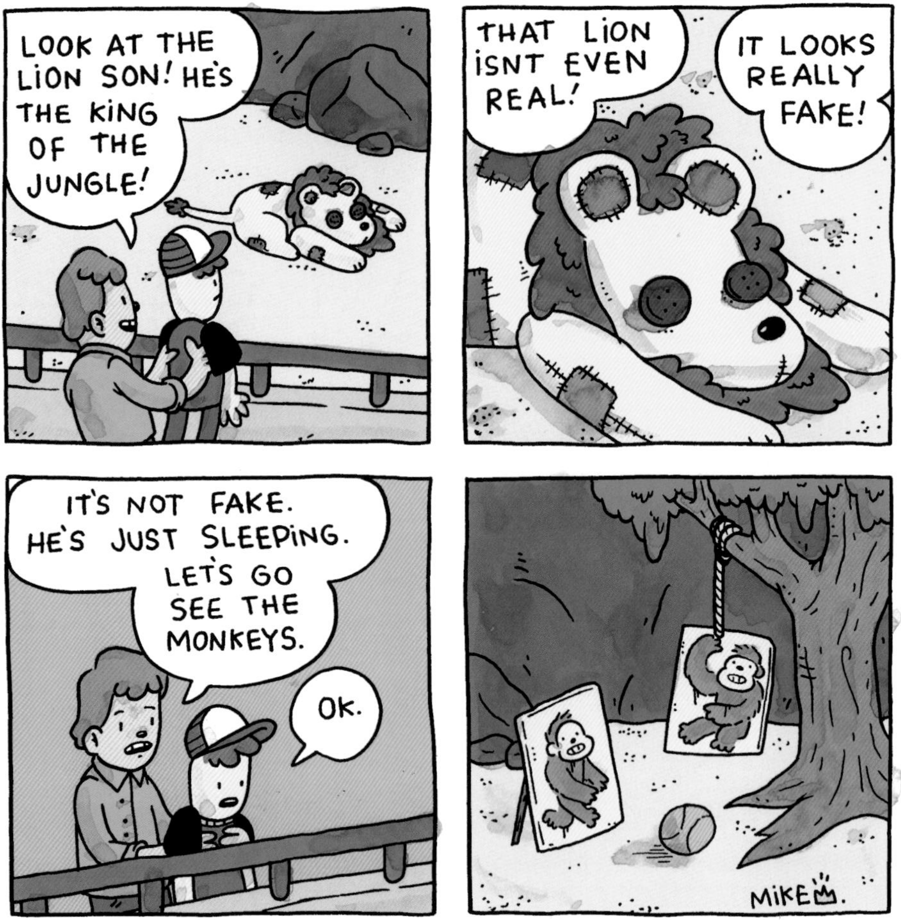
LOOK AT THE LION SON! HE'S THE KING OF THE JUNGLE!
THAT LION ISNT EVEN REAL!
IT LOOKS REALLY FAKE!
IT'S NOT FAKE. HE'S JUST SLEEPING.
LET'S GO SEE THE MONKEYS.
OK.
MIKE

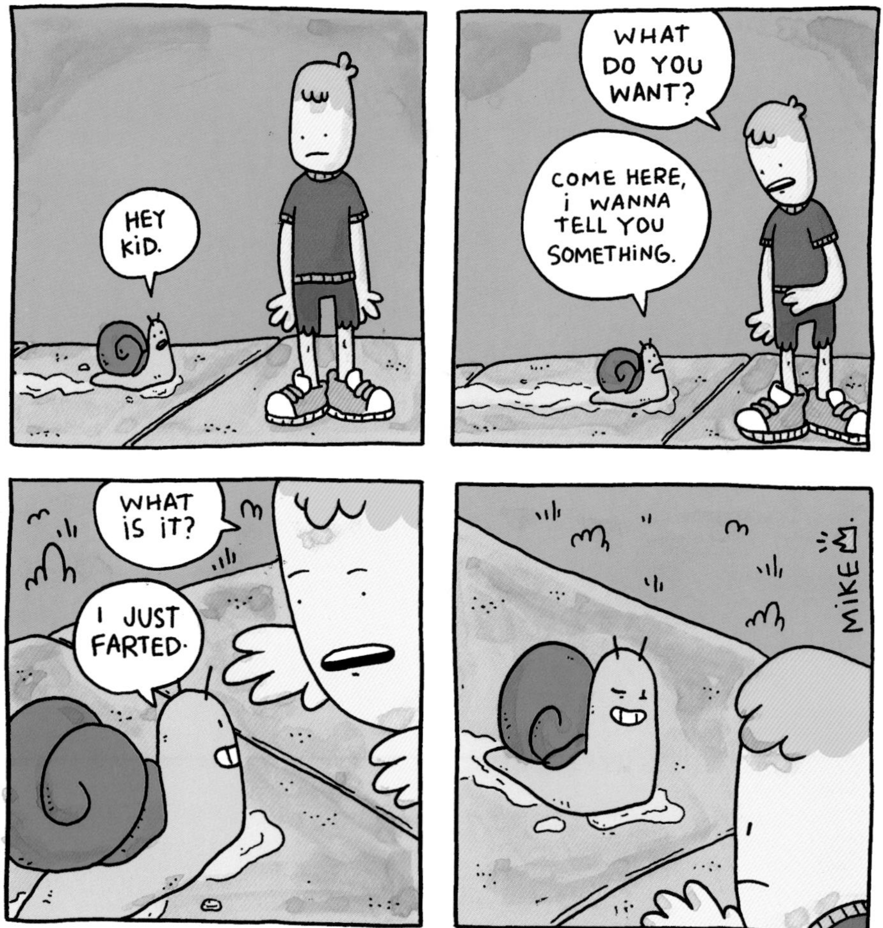
HEY KID.
WHAT DO YOU WANT?
COME HERE, I WANNA TELL YOU SOMETHING.
WHAT IS IT?
I JUST FARTED.
MIKE

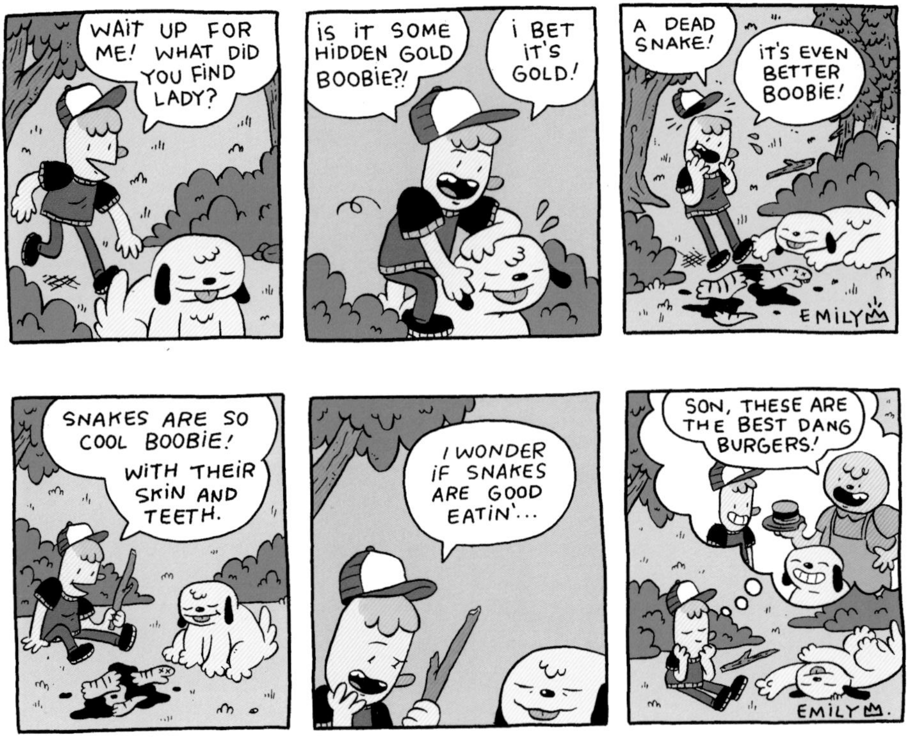
WAIT UP FOR ME! WHAT DID YOU FIND LADY?
IS IT SOME HIDDEN GOLD BOOBIE?!
I BET IT'S GOLD!
A DEAD SNAKE!
IT'S EVEN BETTER BOOBIE!
EMILY
SNAKES ARE SO COOL BOOBIE!
WITH THEIR SKIN AND TEETH.
I WONDER IF SNAKES ARE GOOD EATIN'...
SON, THESE ARE THE BEST DANG BURGERS!
EMILY.

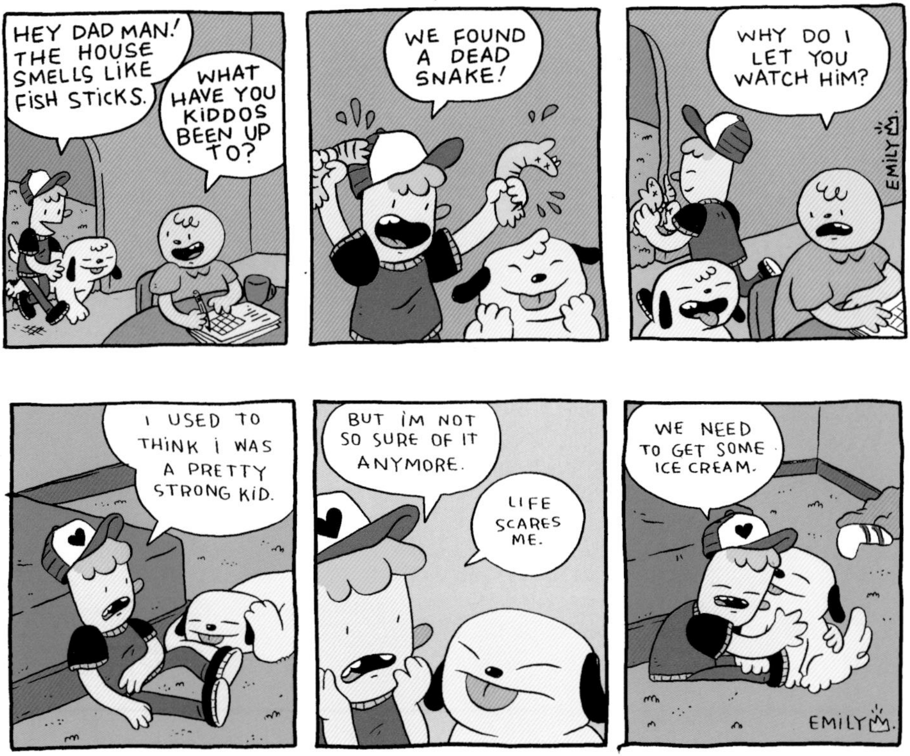
HEY DAD MAN! THE HOUSE SMELLS LIKE FISH STICKS.
WHAT HAVE YOU KIDDOS BEEN UP TO?
WE FOUND A DEAD SNAKE!
WHY DO I LET YOU WATCH HIM?
EMILY
I USED TO THINK I WAS A PRETTY STRONG KID.
BUT IM NOT SO SURE OF IT ANYMORE.
LIFE SCARES ME.
WE NEED TO GET SOME ICE CREAM.
EMILY

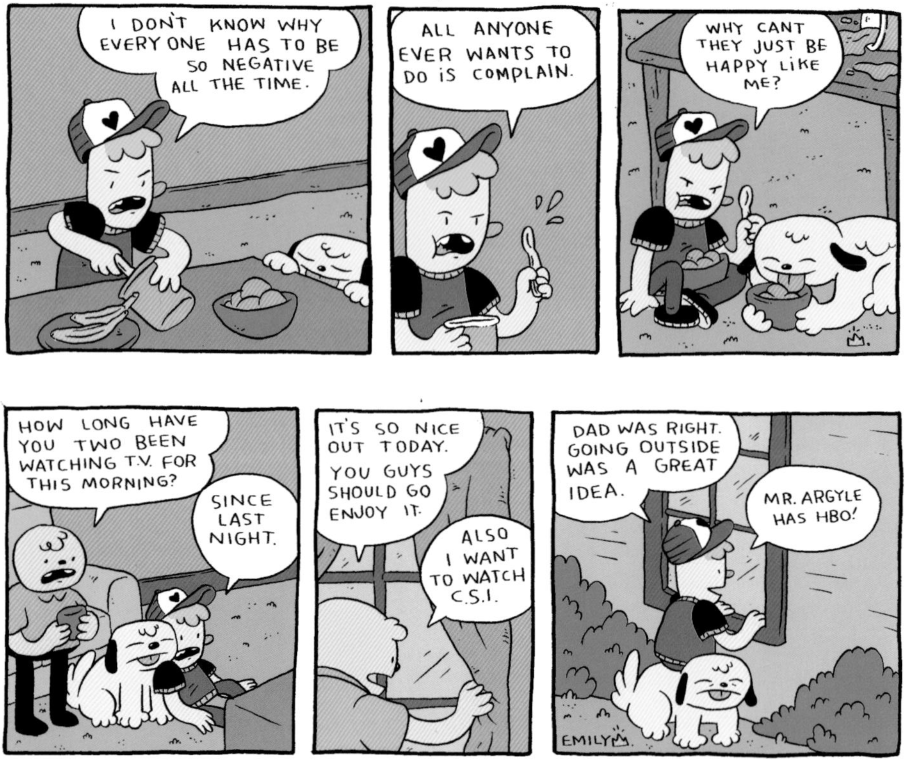
I DON'T KNOW WHY EVERYONE HAS TO BE SO NEGATIVE ALL THE TIME.
ALL ANYONE EVER WANTS TO DO IS COMPLAIN.
WHY CANT THEY JUST BE HAPPY LIKE ME?
HOW LONG HAVE YOU TWO BEEN WATCHING T.V. FOR THIS MORNING?
SINCE LAST NIGHT.
IT'S SO NICE OUT TODAY.
YOU GUYS SHOULD GO ENJOY IT.
ALSO I WANT TO WATCH C.S.I.
DAD WAS RIGHT. GOING OUTSIDE WAS A GREAT IDEA.
MR. ARGYLE HAS HBO!
EMILY

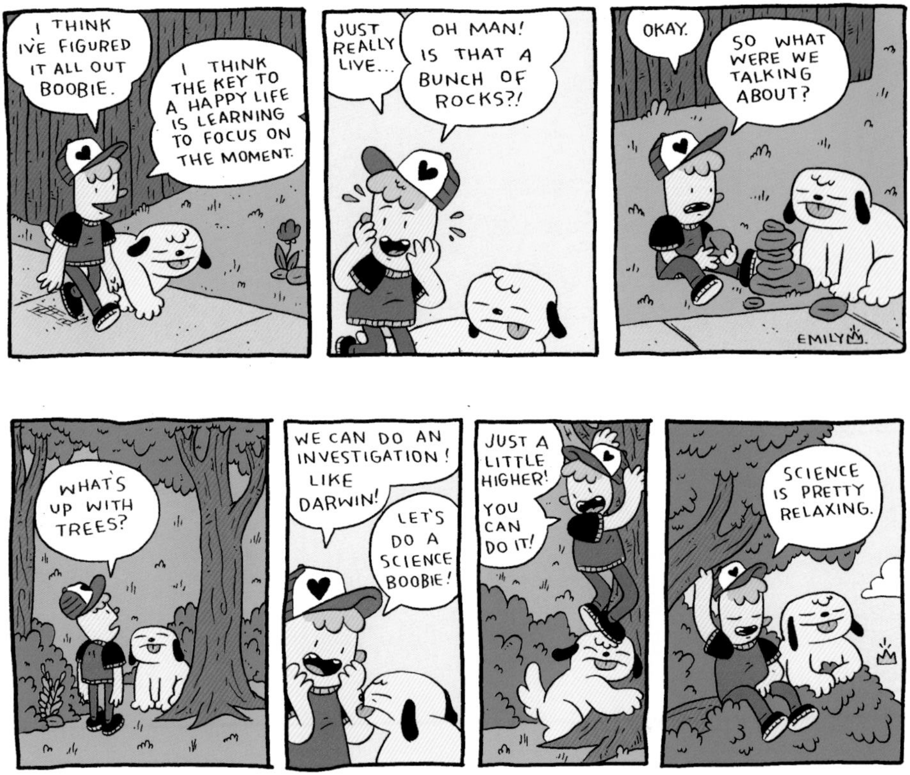
I THINK I'VE FIGURED IT ALL OUT BOOBIE.
I THINK THE KEY TO A HAPPY LIFE IS LEARNING TO FOCUS ON THE MOMENT.
JUST REALLY LIVE...
OH MAN! IS THAT A BUNCH OF ROCKS?!
OKAY.
SO WHAT WERE WE TALKING ABOUT?
EMILY
WHAT'S UP WITH TREES?
WE CAN DO AN INVESTIGATION! LIKE DARWIN!
LET'S DO A SCIENCE BOOBIE!
JUST A LITTLE HIGHER!
YOU CAN DO IT!
SCIENCE IS PRETTY RELAXING.

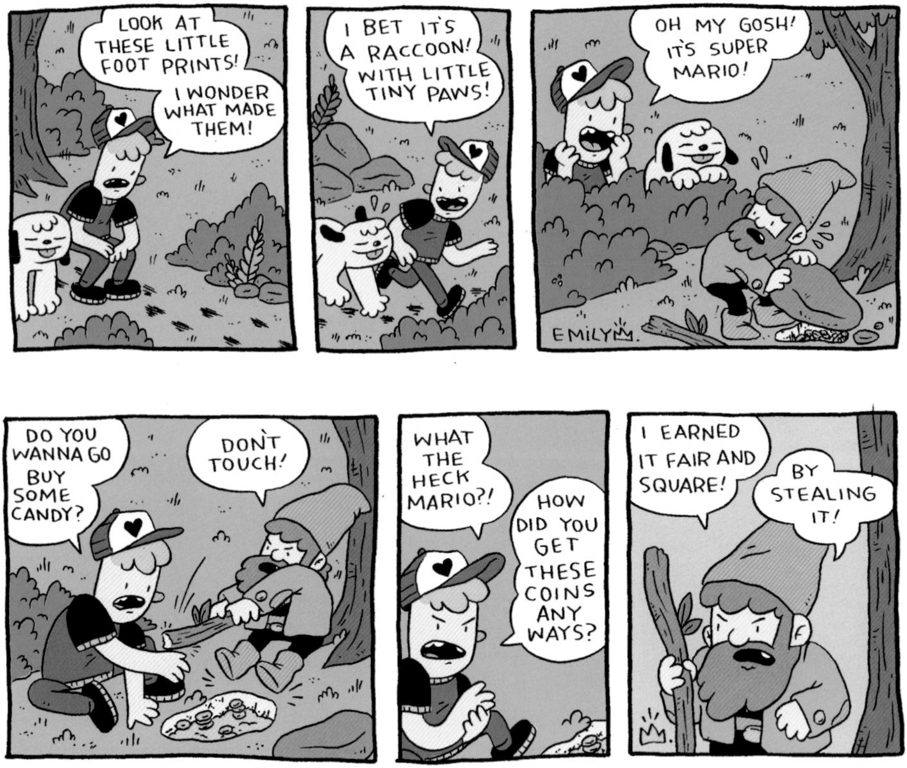
LOOK AT THESE LITTLE FOOT PRINTS!
I WONDER WHAT MADE THEM!
I BET IT'S A RACCOON! WITH LITTLE TINY PAWS!
OH MY GOSH! IT'S SUPER MARIO!
EMILY
DO YOU WANNA GO BUY SOME CANDY?
DON'T TOUCH!
WHAT THE HECK MARIO?!
HOW DID YOU GET THESE COINS ANY WAYS?
I EARNED IT FAIR AND SQUARE!
BY STEALING IT!

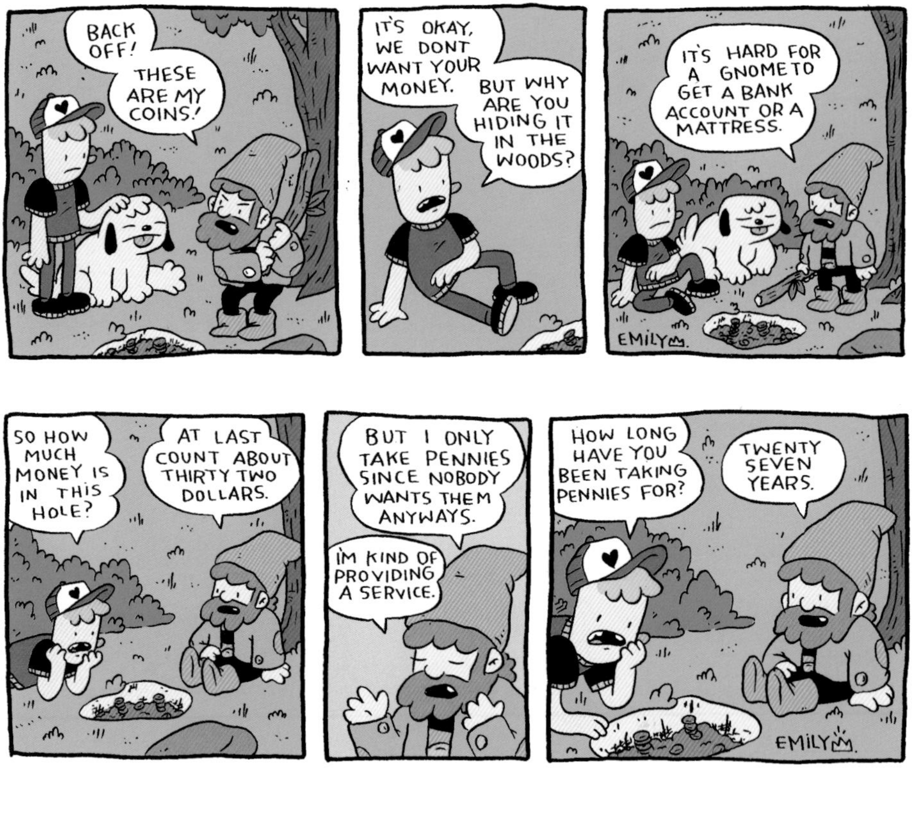
BACK OFF!
THESE ARE MY COINS!
IT'S OKAY, WE DONT WANT YOUR MONEY.
BUT WHY ARE YOU HIDING IT IN THE WOODS?
IT'S HARD FOR A GNOME TO GET A BANK ACCOUNT OR A MATTRESS.
EMILY
SO HOW MUCH MONEY IS IN THIS HOLE?
AT LAST COUNT ABOUT THIRTY TWO DOLLARS.
BUT I ONLY TAKE PENNIES SINCE NOBODY WANTS THEM ANYWAYS.
I'M KIND OF PROVIDING A SERVICE.
HOW LONG HAVE YOU BEEN TAKING PENNIES FOR?
TWENTY SEVEN YEARS.
EMILY

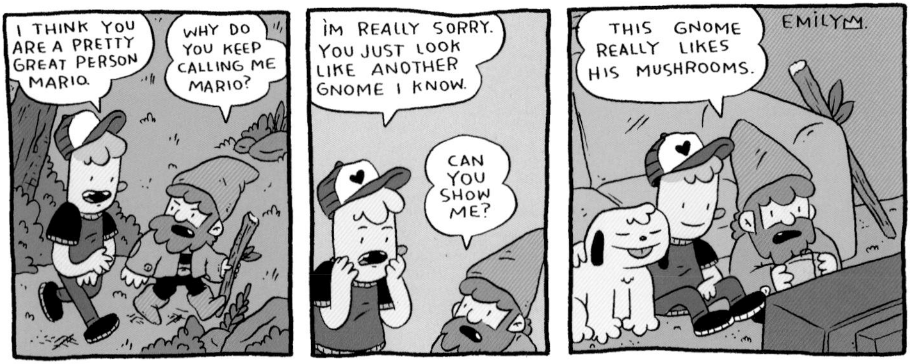
I THINK YOU ARE A PRETTY GREAT PERSON MARIO.
WHY DO YOU KEEP CALLING ME MARIO?
IM REALLY SORRY. YOU JUST LOOK LIKE ANOTHER GNOME I KNOW.
CAN YOU SHOW ME?
THIS GNOME REALLY LIKES HIS MUSHROOMS.
EMILY

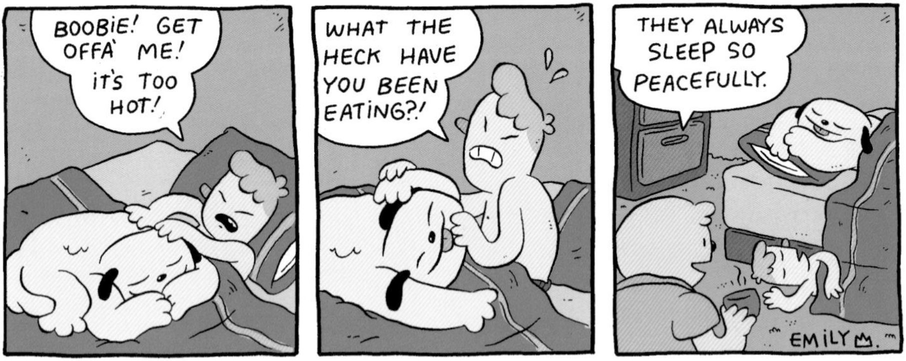
BOOBIE! GET OFFA' ME! IT'S TOO HOT!
WHAT THE HECK HAVE YOU BEEN EATING?!
THEY ALWAYS SLEEP SO PEACEFULLY.
EMILY

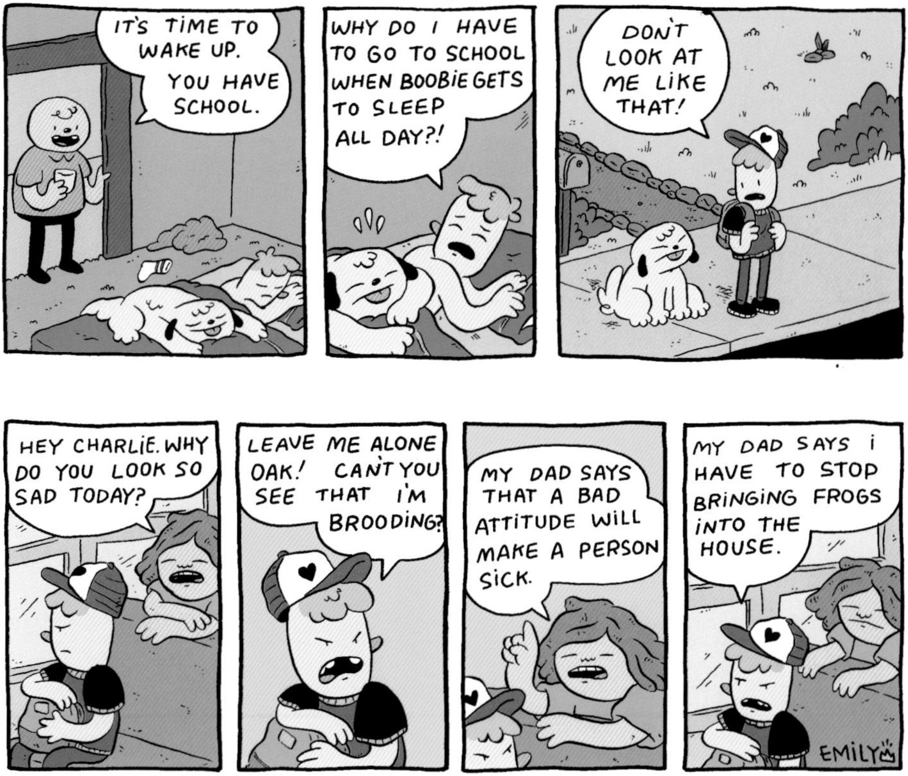
IT'S TIME TO WAKE UP.
YOU HAVE SCHOOL.
WHY DO I HAVE TO GO TO SCHOOL WHEN BOOBIE GETS TO SLEEP ALL DAY?!
DON'T LOOK AT ME LIKE THAT!
HEY CHARLIE. WHY DO YOU LOOK SO SAD TODAY?
LEAVE ME ALONE OAK! CAN'T YOU SEE THAT I'M BROODING?
MY DAD SAYS THAT A BAD ATTITUDE WILL MAKE A PERSON SICK.
MY DAD SAYS I HAVE TO STOP BRINGING FROGS INTO THE HOUSE.
EMILY

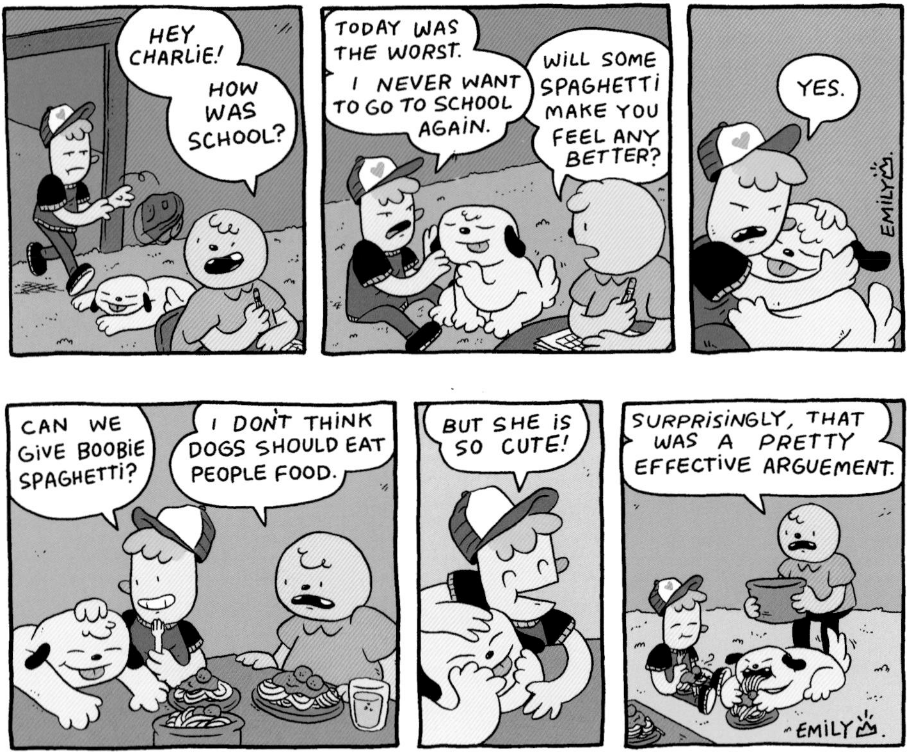
HEY CHARLIE!
HOW WAS SCHOOL?
TODAY WAS THE WORST.
I NEVER WANT TO GO TO SCHOOL AGAIN.
WILL SOME SPAGHETTI MAKE YOU FEEL ANY BETTER?
YES.
EMILY
CAN WE GIVE BOOBIE SPAGHETTI?
I DON'T THINK DOGS SHOULD EAT PEOPLE FOOD.
BUT SHE IS SO CUTE!
SURPRISINGLY, THAT WAS A PRETTY EFFECTIVE ARGUEMENT.
EMILY

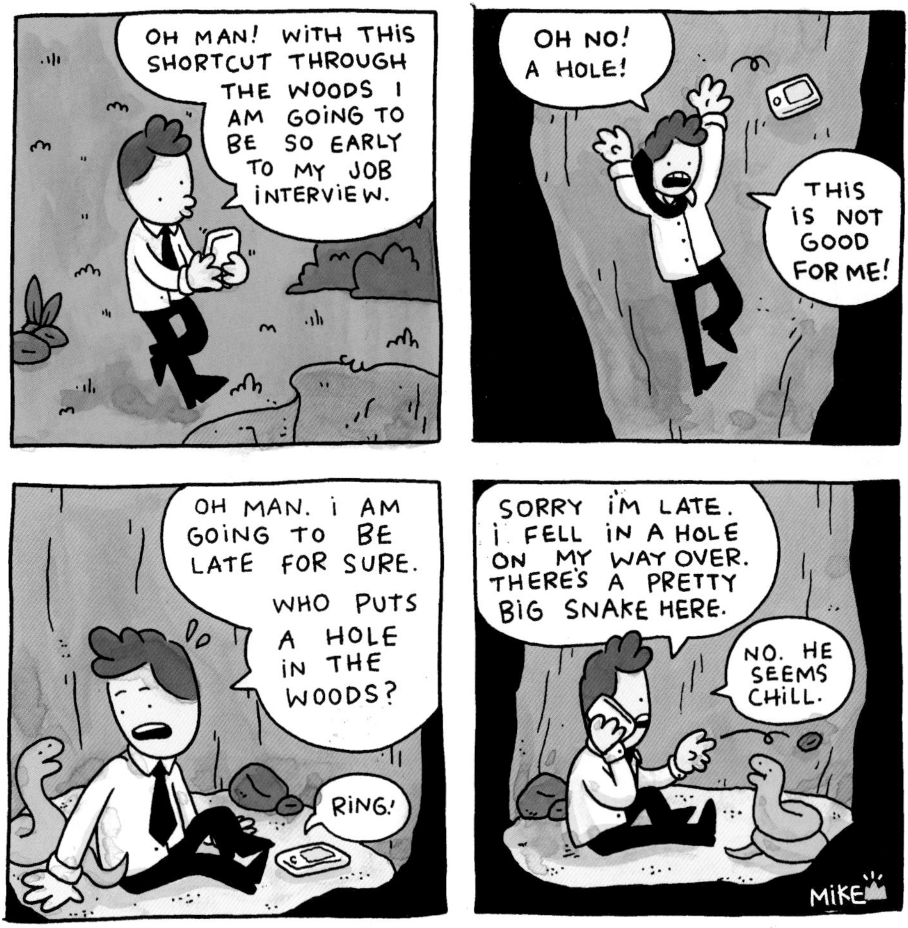
OH MAN! WITH THIS SHORTCUT THROUGH THE WOODS I AM GOING TO BE SO EARLY TO MY JOB INTERVIEW.
OH NO! A HOLE!
THIS IS NOT GOOD FOR ME!
OH MAN. I AM GOING TO BE LATE FOR SURE.
WHO PUTS A HOLE IN THE WOODS?
RING!
SORRY I'M LATE. I FELL IN A HOLE ON MY WAY OVER. THERE'S A PRETTY BIG SNAKE HERE.
NO. HE SEEMS CHILL.
MIKE

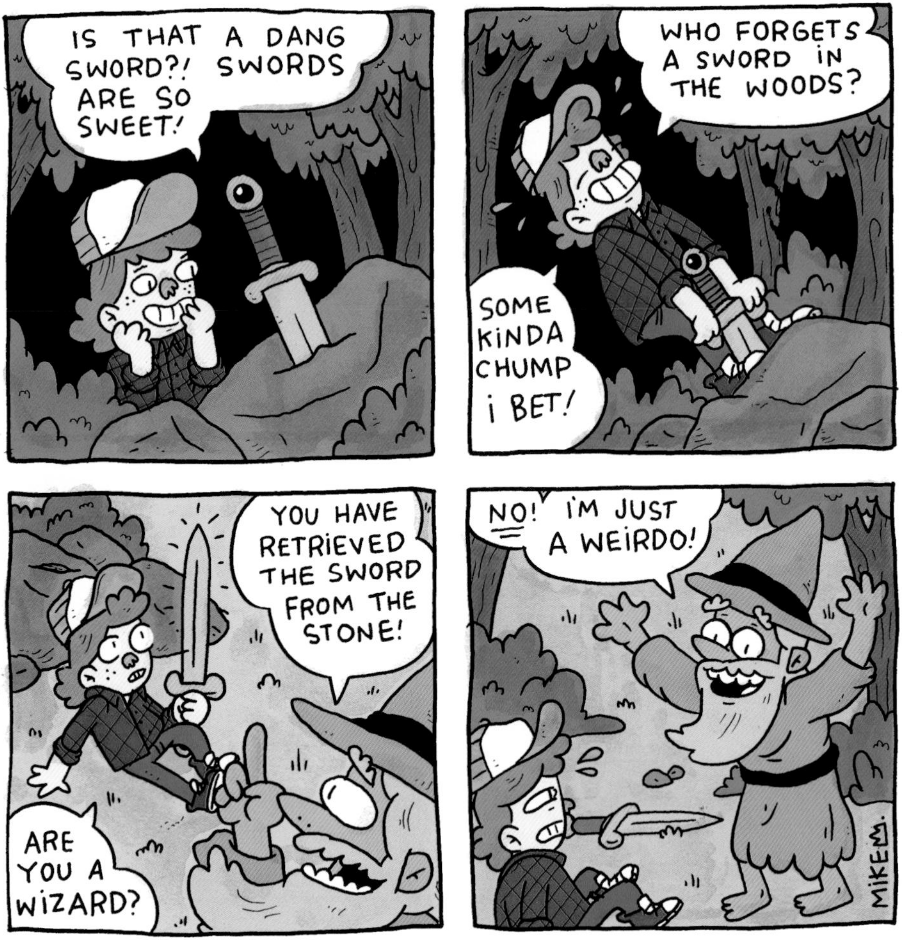
IS THAT A DANG SWORD?! SWORDS ARE SO SWEET!
WHO FORGETS A SWORD IN THE WOODS?
SOME KINDA CHUMP I BET!
YOU HAVE RETRIEVED THE SWORD FROM THE STONE!
ARE YOU A WIZARD?
NO! I'M JUST A WEIRDO!
MIKEM.

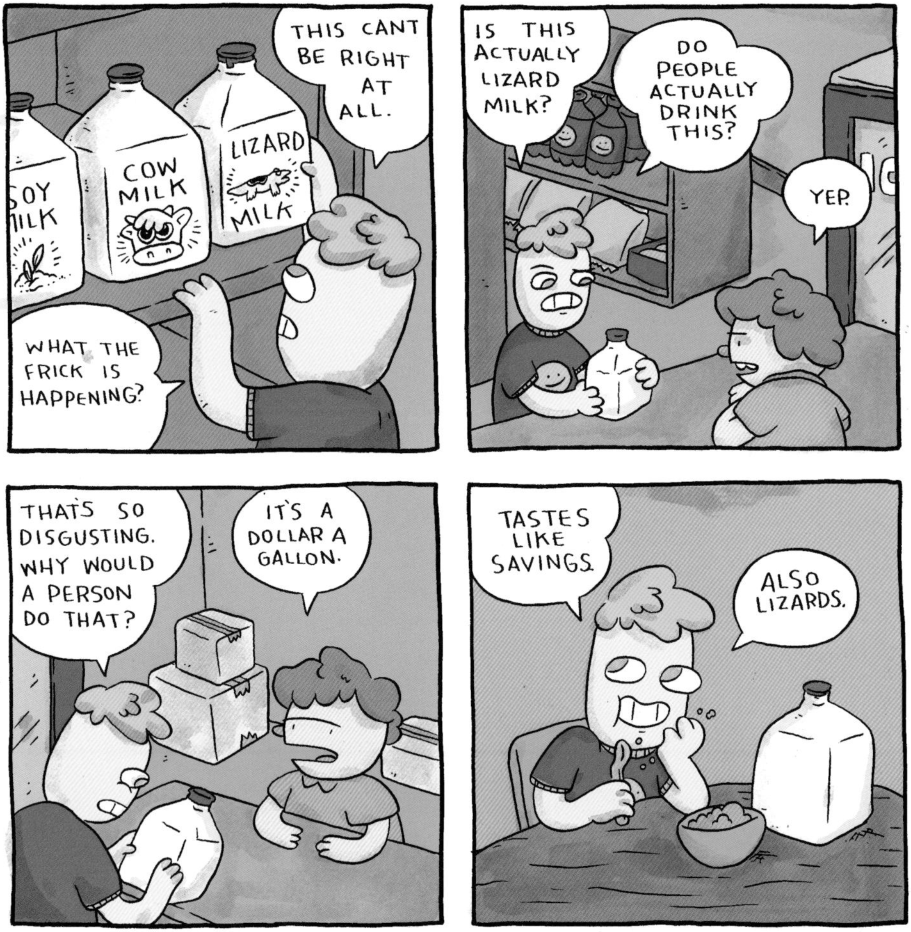
THIS CANT BE RIGHT AT ALL.
SOY MILK
COW MILK
LIZARD MILK
WHAT THE FRICK IS HAPPENING?
IS THIS ACTUALLY LIZARD MILK?
DO PEOPLE ACTUALLY DRINK THIS?
YEP.
THAT'S SO DISGUSTING. WHY WOULD A PERSON DO THAT?
IT'S A DOLLAR A GALLON.
TASTES LIKE SAVINGS.
ALSO LIZARDS.

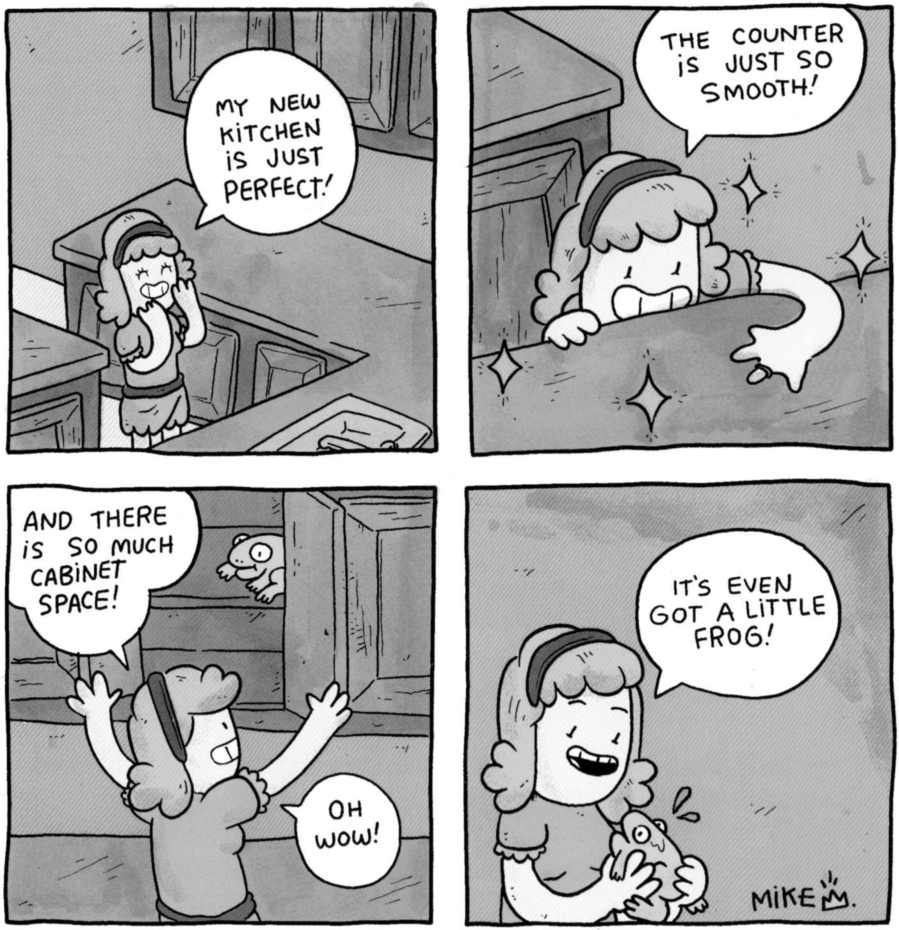
MY NEW KITCHEN IS JUST PERFECT!
THE COUNTER IS JUST SO SMOOTH!
AND THERE IS SO MUCH CABINET SPACE!
OH WOW!
IT'S EVEN GOT A LITTLE FROG!
MIKE M.

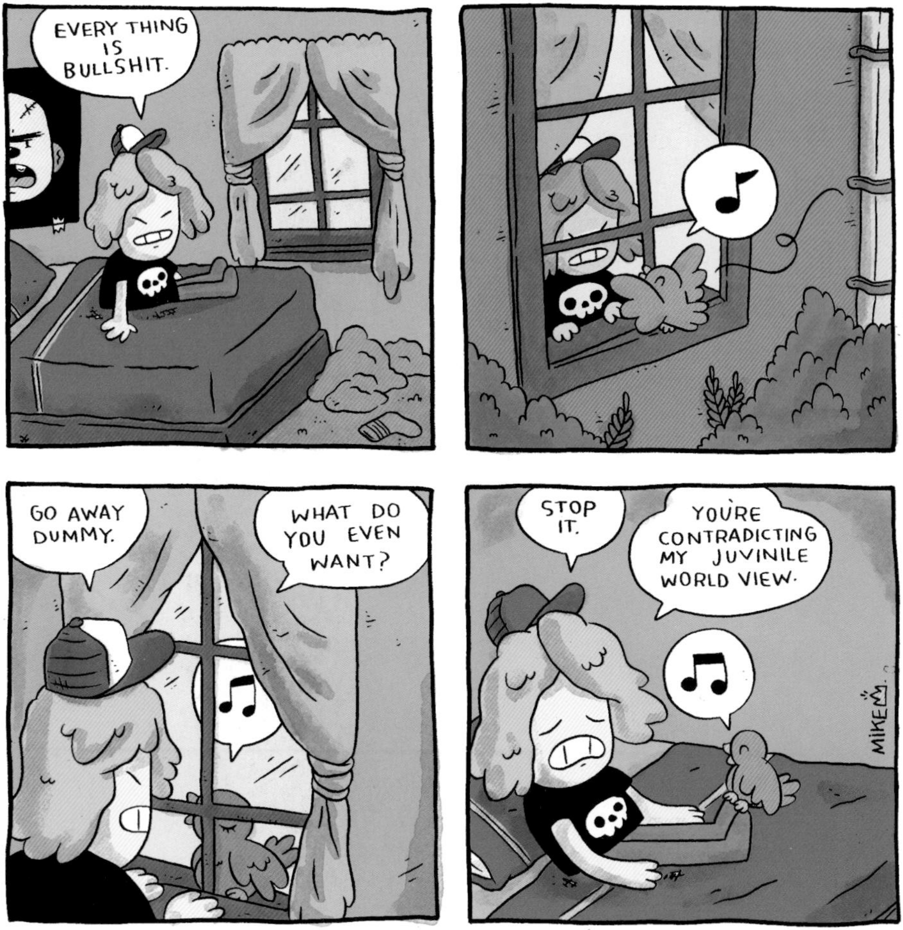
EVERY THING IS BULLSHIT.
GO AWAY DUMMY.
WHAT DO YOU EVEN WANT?
STOP IT.
YOU'RE CONTRADICTING MY JUVINILE WORLD VIEW.
MIKE

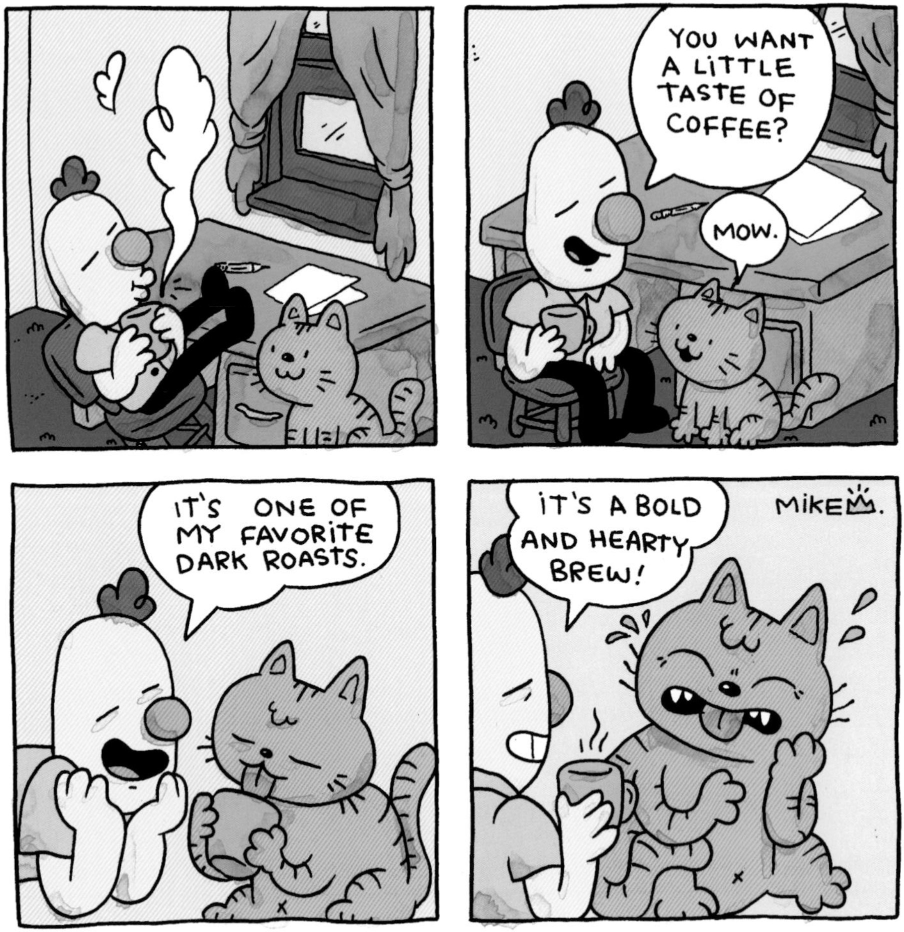
YOU WANT A LITTLE TASTE OF COFFEE?
MOW.
IT'S ONE OF MY FAVORITE DARK ROASTS.
IT'S A BOLD AND HEARTY BREW!
MIKE M.

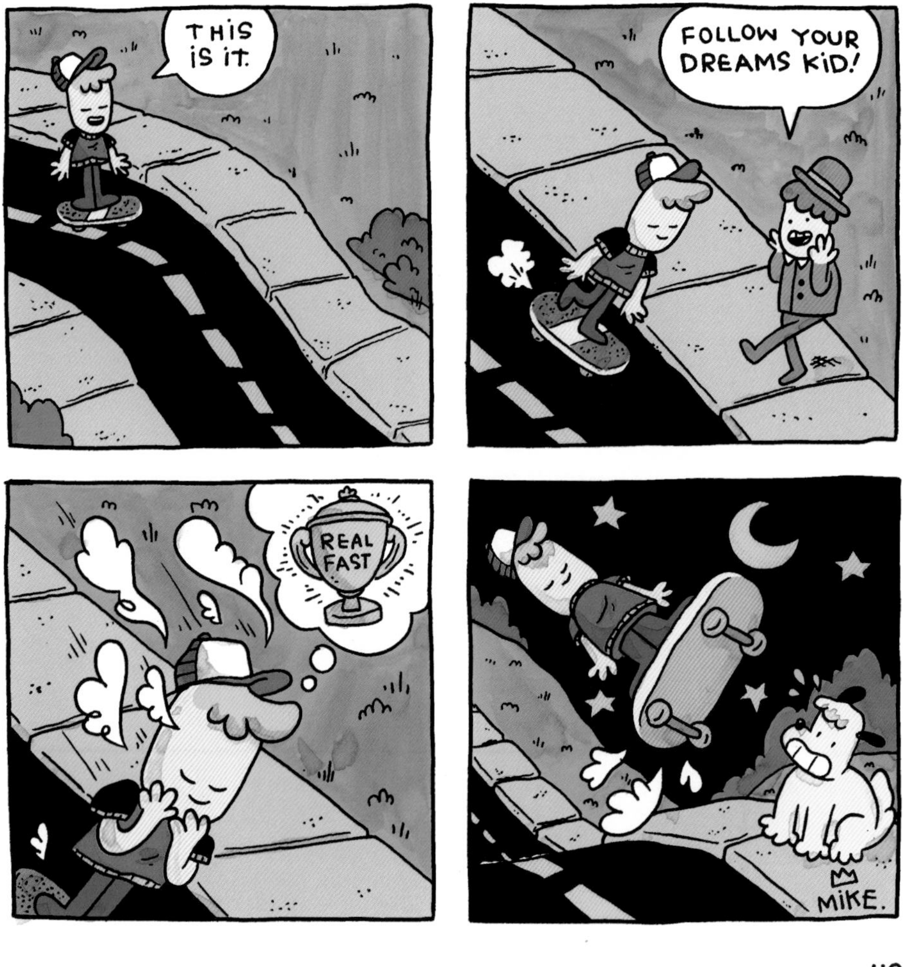
THIS IS IT.
FOLLOW YOUR DREAMS KID!
REAL FAST
MIKE.

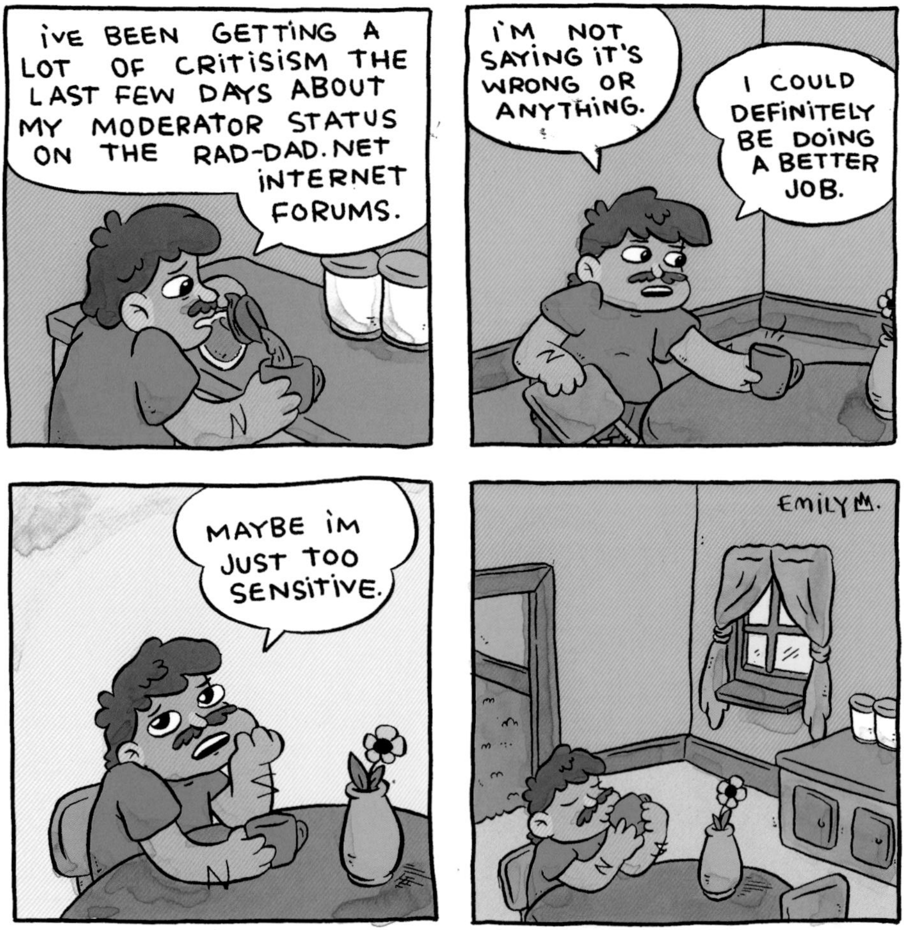

iVE BEEN GETTING A LOT OF CRITISISM THE LAST FEW DAYS ABOUT MY MODERATOR STATUS ON THE RAD-DAD.NET INTERNET FORUMS.
I'M NOT SAYING IT'S WRONG OR ANYTHING.
I COULD DEFINITELY BE DOING A BETTER JOB.
MAYBE IM JUST TOO SENSITIVE.
EMILY M.

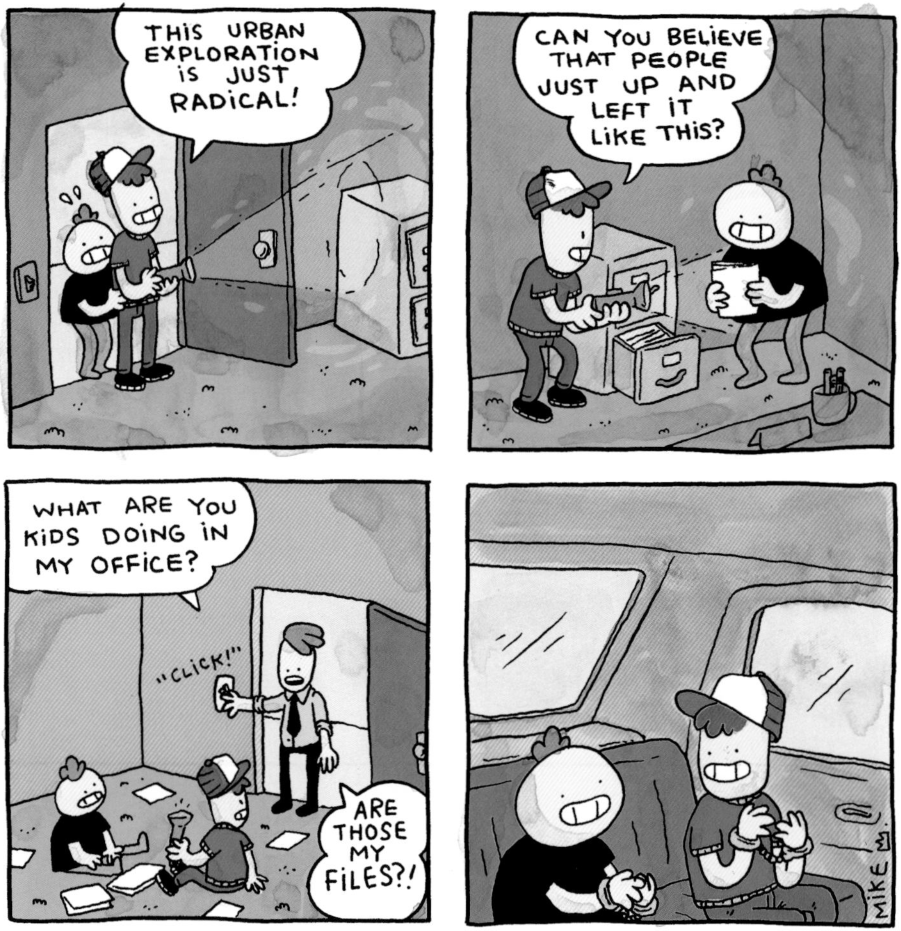
THIS URBAN EXPLORATION IS JUST RADICAL!
CAN YOU BELIEVE THAT PEOPLE JUST UP AND LEFT IT LIKE THIS?
WHAT ARE YOU KIDS DOING IN MY OFFICE?
"CLICK!"
ARE THOSE MY FILES?!
MIKE M.

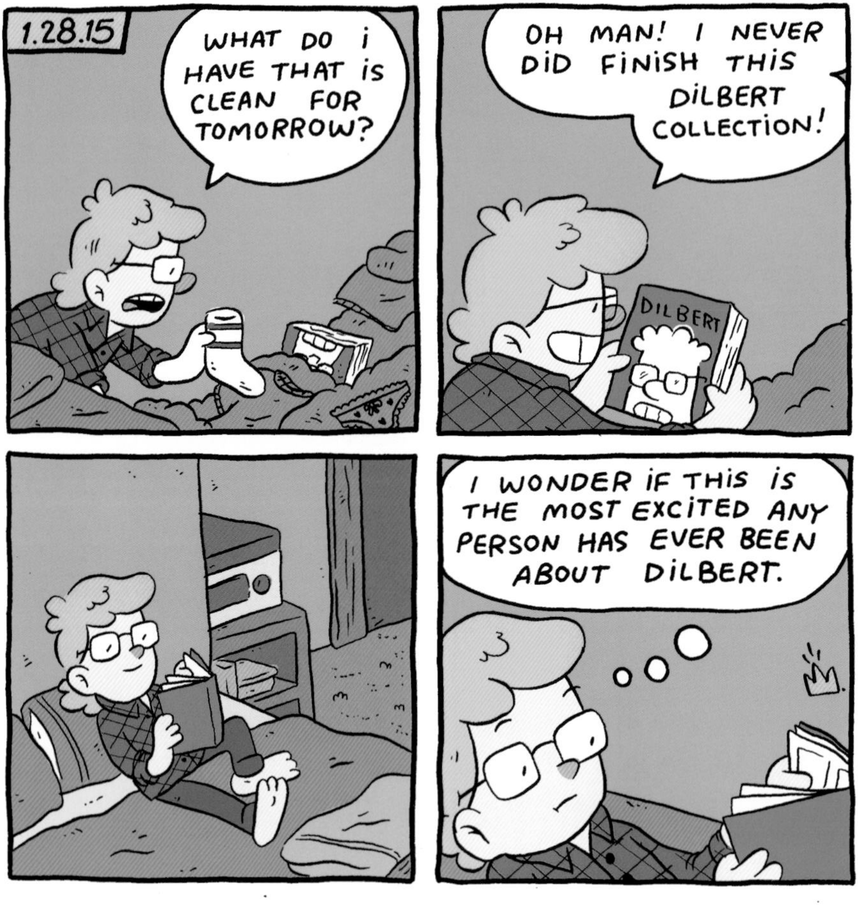
1.28.15
WHAT DO i HAVE THAT iS CLEAN FOR TOMORROW?
OH MAN! I NEVER DiD FiNiSH THiS DiLBERT COLLECTiON!
DILBERT
I WONDER iF THIS iS THE MOST EXCiTED ANY PERSON HAS EVER BEEN ABOUT DiLBERT.

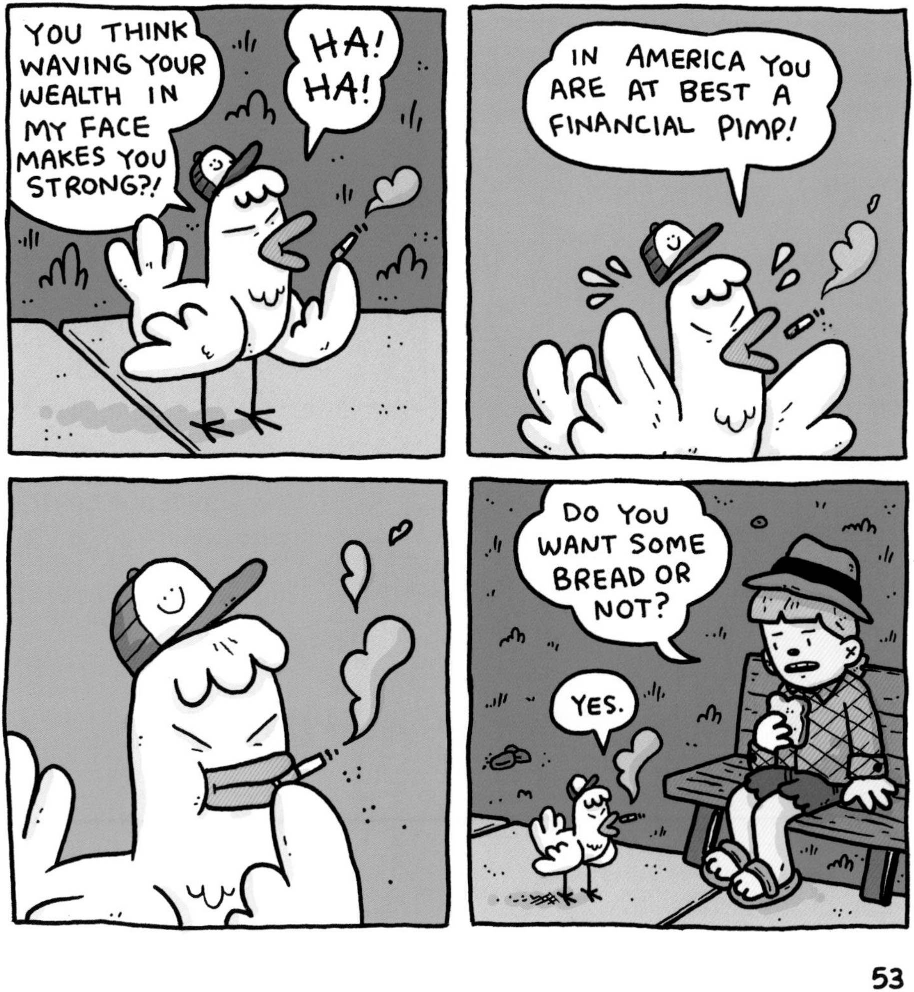
YOU THINK WAVING YOUR WEALTH IN MY FACE MAKES YOU STRONG?!
HA! HA!
IN AMERICA YOU ARE AT BEST A FINANCIAL PIMP!
DO YOU WANT SOME BREAD OR NOT?
YES.

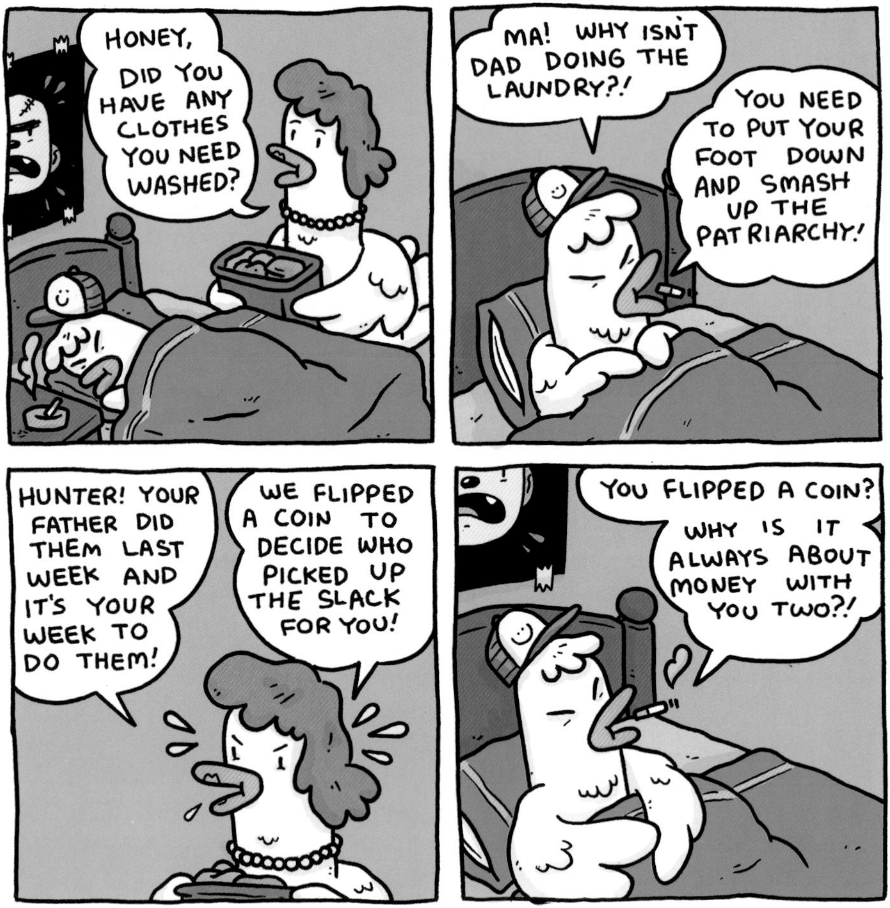
HONEY,
DID YOU HAVE ANY CLOTHES YOU NEED WASHED?
MA! WHY ISN'T DAD DOING THE LAUNDRY?!
YOU NEED TO PUT YOUR FOOT DOWN AND SMASH UP THE PATRIARCHY!
HUNTER! YOUR FATHER DID THEM LAST WEEK AND IT'S YOUR WEEK TO DO THEM!
WE FLIPPED A COIN TO DECIDE WHO PICKED UP THE SLACK FOR YOU!
YOU FLIPPED A COIN?
WHY IS IT ALWAYS ABOUT MONEY WITH YOU TWO?!

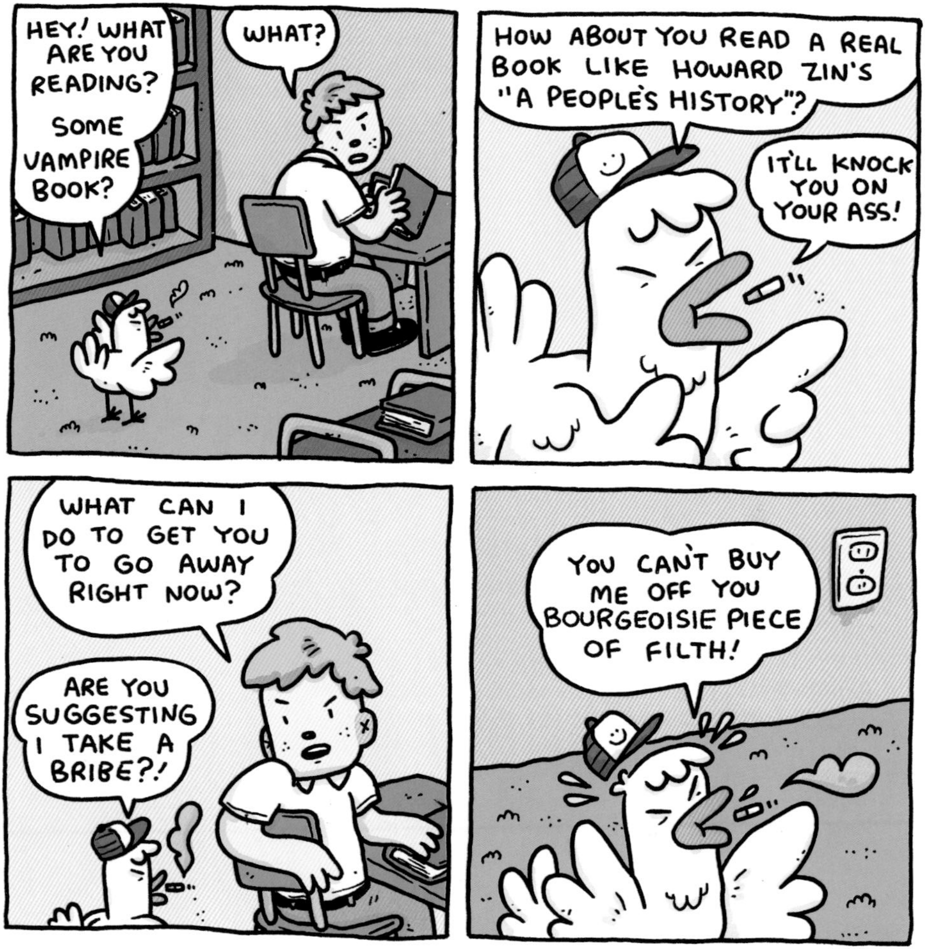
HEY! WHAT ARE YOU READING?
SOME VAMPIRE BOOK?
WHAT?
HOW ABOUT YOU READ A REAL BOOK LIKE HOWARD ZIN'S "A PEOPLE'S HISTORY"?
IT'LL KNOCK YOU ON YOUR ASS!
WHAT CAN I DO TO GET YOU TO GO AWAY RIGHT NOW?
ARE YOU SUGGESTING I TAKE A BRIBE?!
YOU CAN'T BUY ME OFF YOU BOURGEOISIE PIECE OF FILTH!

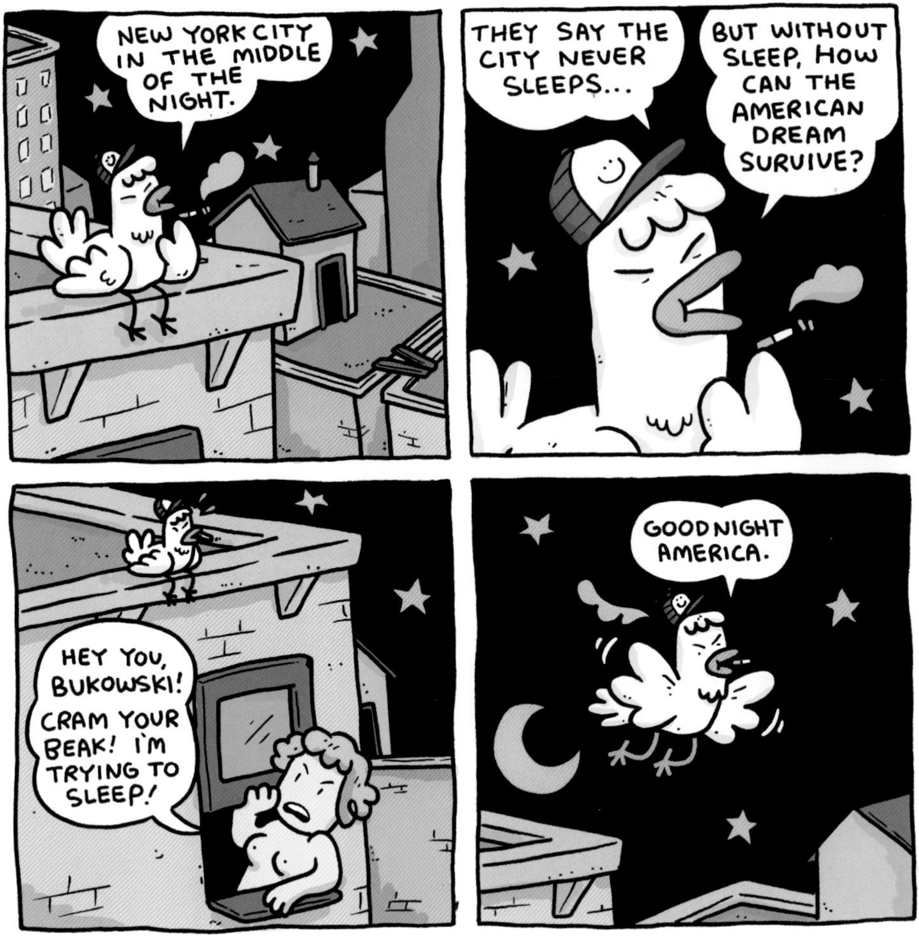
NEW YORK CITY IN THE MIDDLE OF THE NIGHT.
THEY SAY THE CITY NEVER SLEEPS...
BUT WITHOUT SLEEP, HOW CAN THE AMERICAN DREAM SURVIVE?
HEY YOU, BUKOWSKI!
CRAM YOUR BEAK! I'M TRYING TO SLEEP!
GOODNIGHT AMERICA.

THESE ARE DESIGNS FOR TATTOOS
I THINK WOULD BE AWESOME.

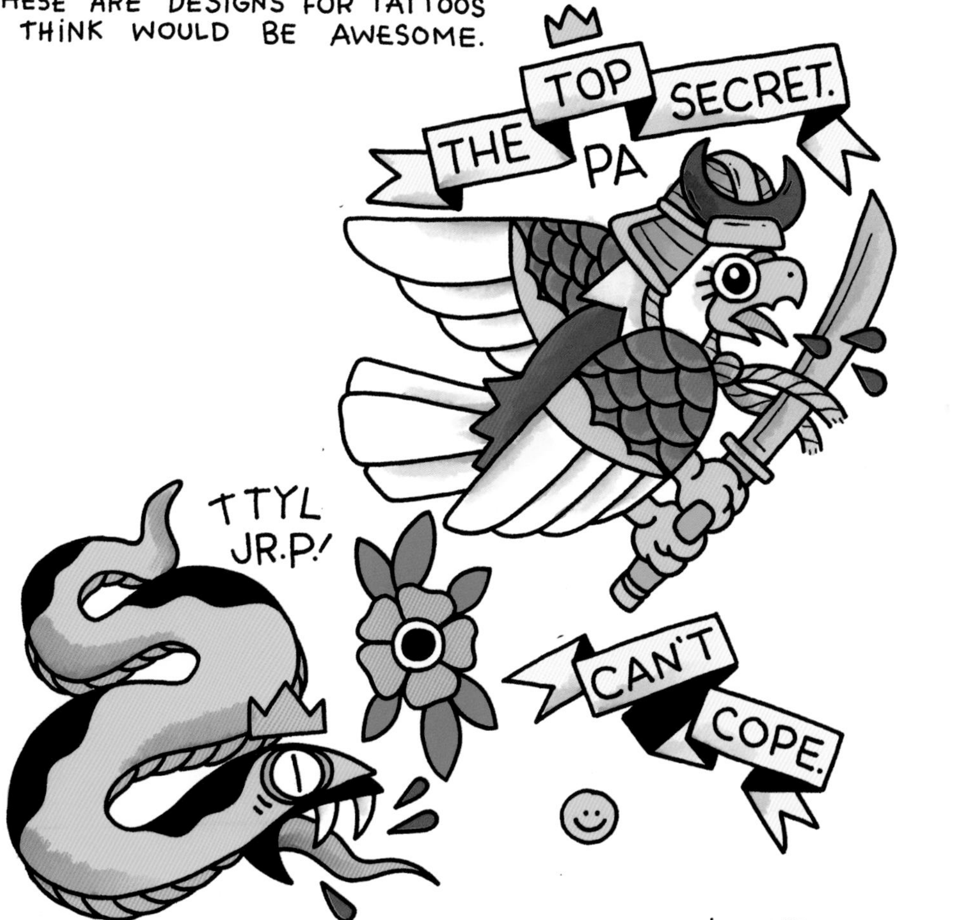
THE TOP SECRET.
PA
TTYL
JR.P!
CAN'T COPE.

PLEASE FIND A LICENCED ARTIST.
(OR JUST COME LET ME DO IT!)

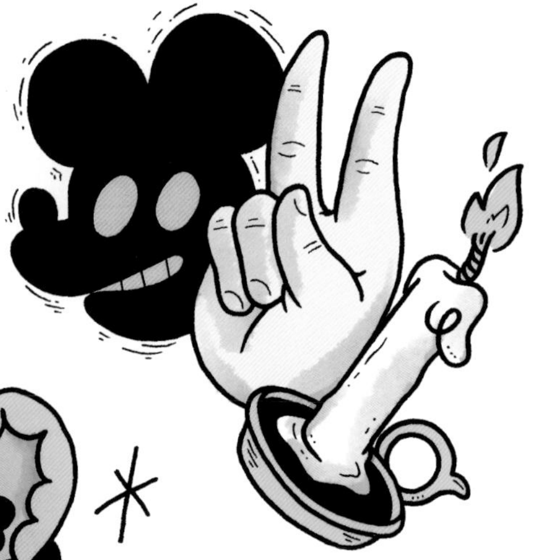

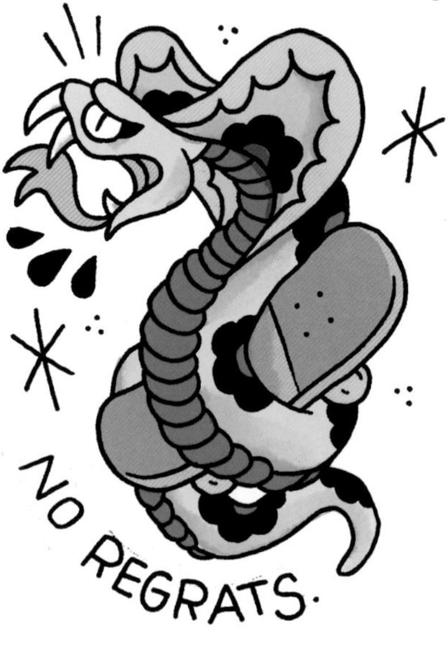
NO REGRATS.

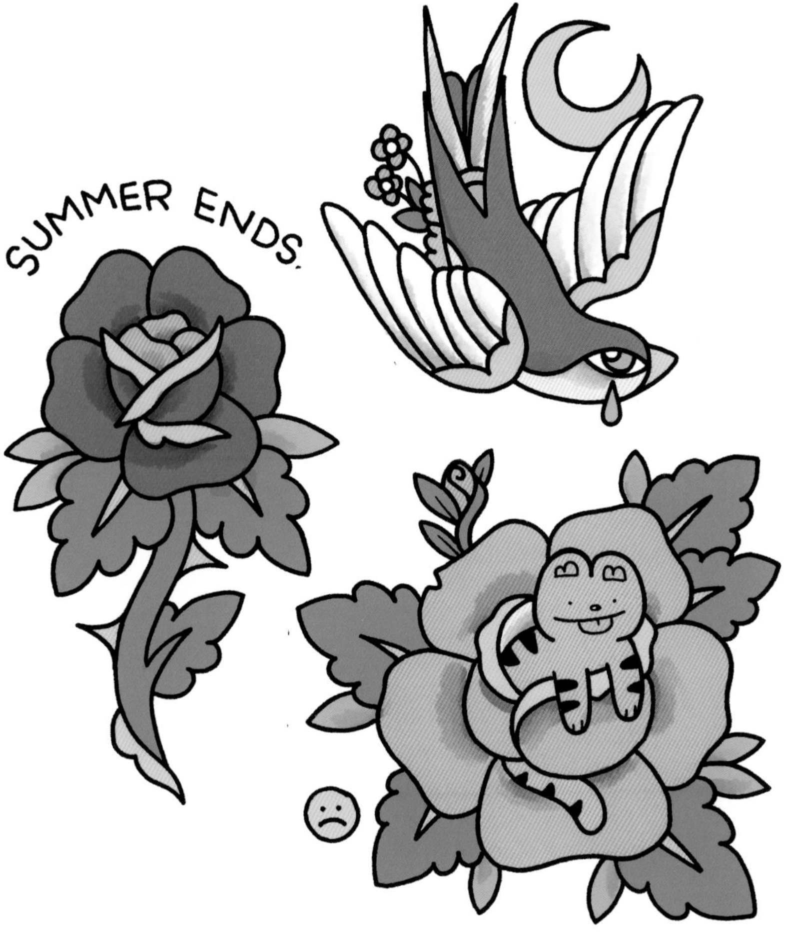
SUMMER ENDS.

THANK YOU FOR READING MY BOOK!!!

SECOND PRINTING MADE POSSIBLE BY READERS LIKE YOU!

NEVER GIVE UP EVER.

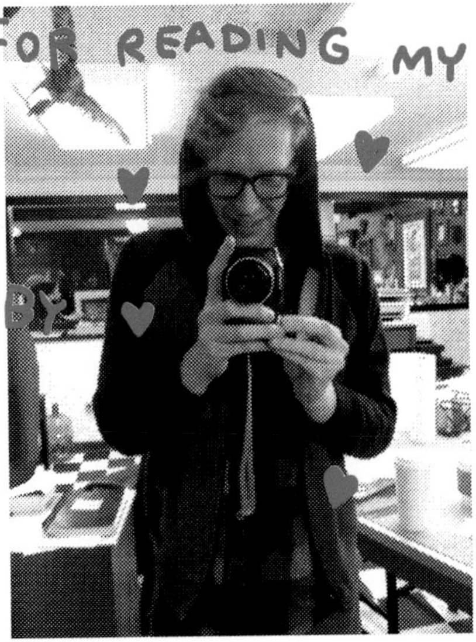

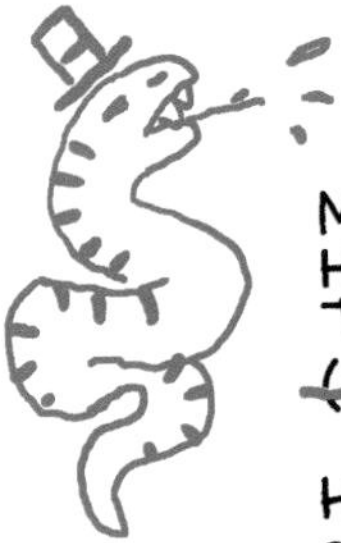

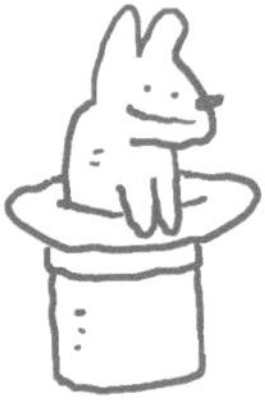

MIKE KING LIVES IN THE WOODS WITH HIS TWO DOGS AND SIX CATS. HE TATTOOS AT ~~SUPERNOVA TATTOO. (30 N. BLOCK AVE. FAYETTEVILLE, AR.)~~ NOT ANYMORE!

HE HAS SELF PUBLISHED OVER 1,000 PAGES OF HIS NOW FINISHED ZINE "LION'S TEETH." THIS BOOK IS MOSTLY STUFF HE FORGOT TO SCAN.

IT'S MICHAELSWEATER.COM!

IF YOU ENJOYED THIS BOOK YOU SHOULD SIGN UP FOR THE MAILING LIST AT- ~~PLEASEKEEPWARM.COM~~

MAILING LIST NO LONGER EXISTS!

MORE TREASURE FROM SILVER SPROCKET

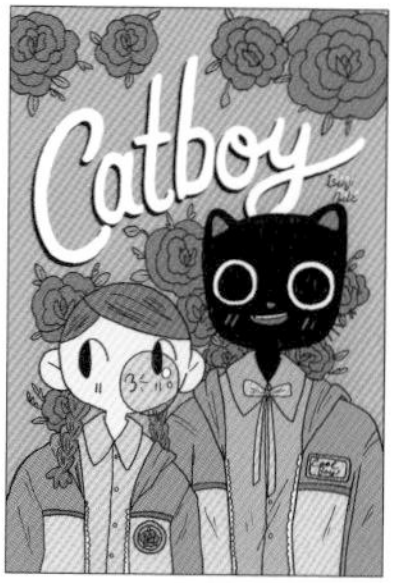
Catboy

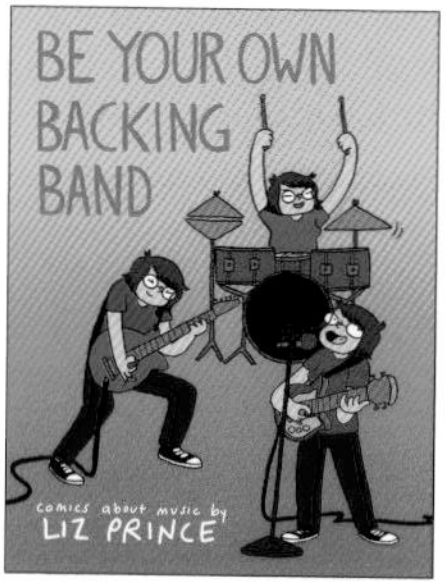
BE YOUR OWN
BACKING
BAND
comics about music by
LIZ PRINCE

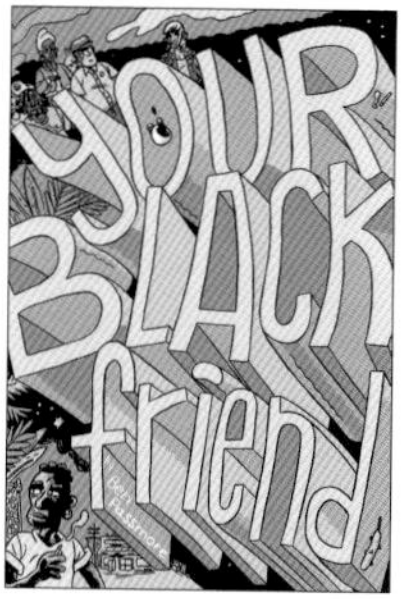
your
BLACK
friend

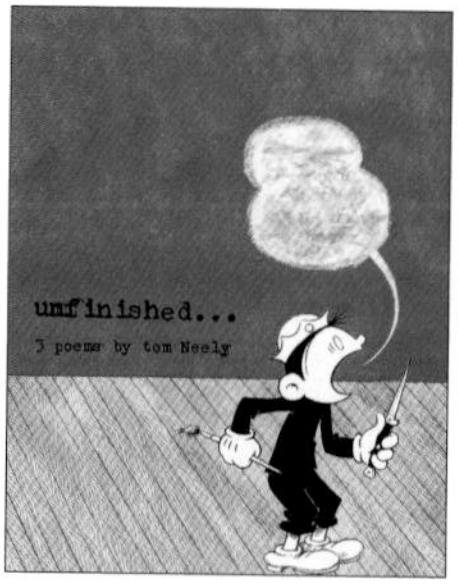
unfinished...
3 poems by tom Neely

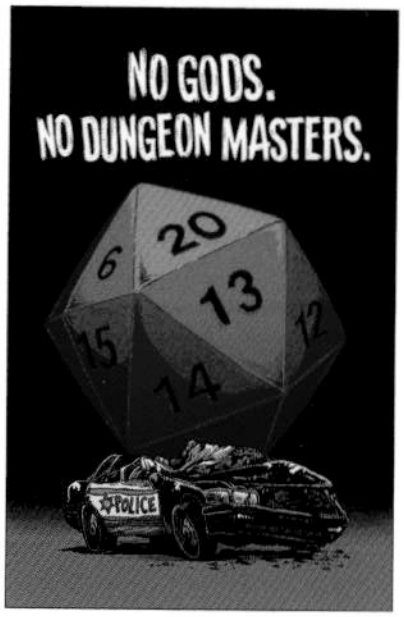
NO GODS.
NO DUNGEON MASTERS.
POLICE

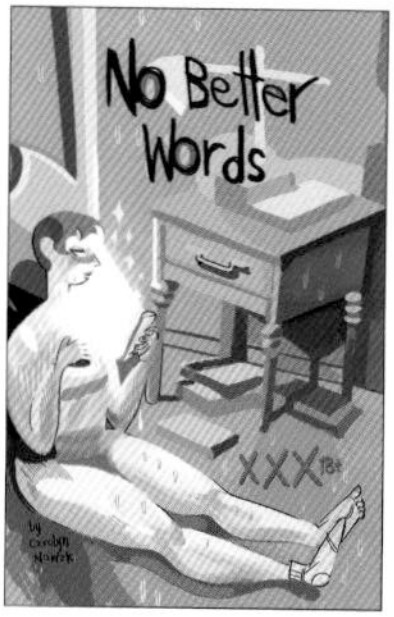
No Better
Words
XXX 18+

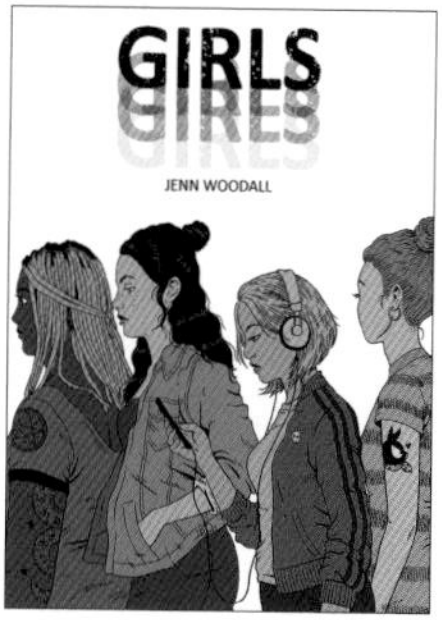
GIRLS
JENN WOODALL

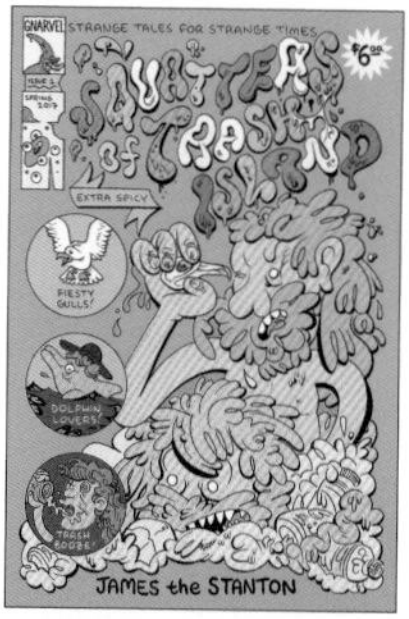
STRANGE TALES FOR STRANGE TIMES
EXTRA SPICY
JAMES the STANTON

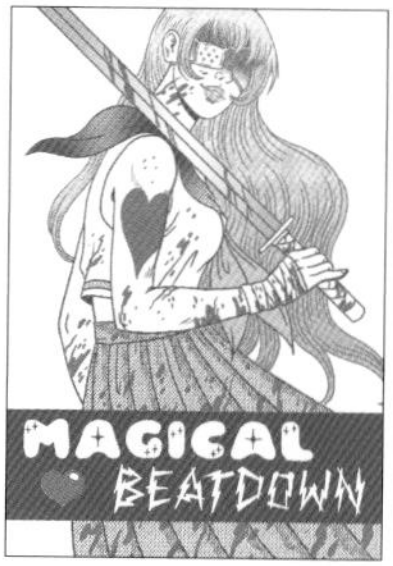
MAGICAL
BEATDOWN

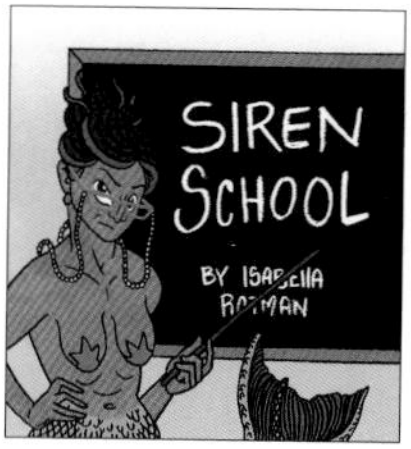
SIREN
SCHOOL

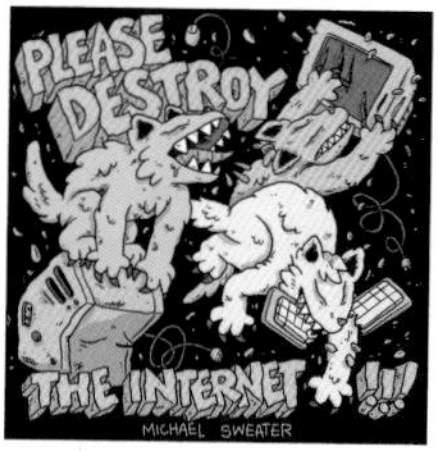
PLEASE
DESTROY
THE INTERNET !!!
MICHAEL SWEATER

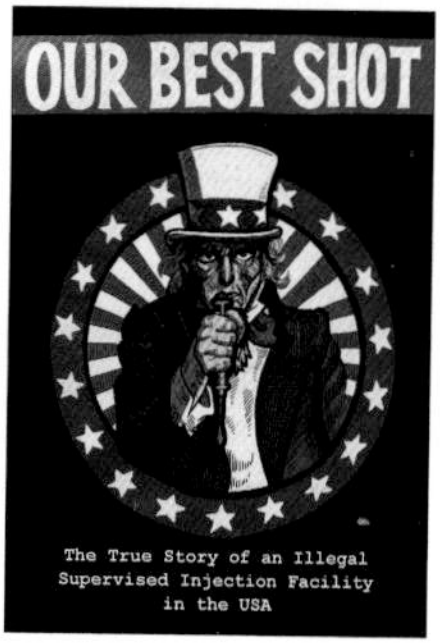
OUR BEST SHOT
The True Story of an Illegal
Supervised Injection Facility
in the USA

WWW.SILVERSPROCKET.NET

ALSO AVAILABLE FROM MICHAEL SWEATER

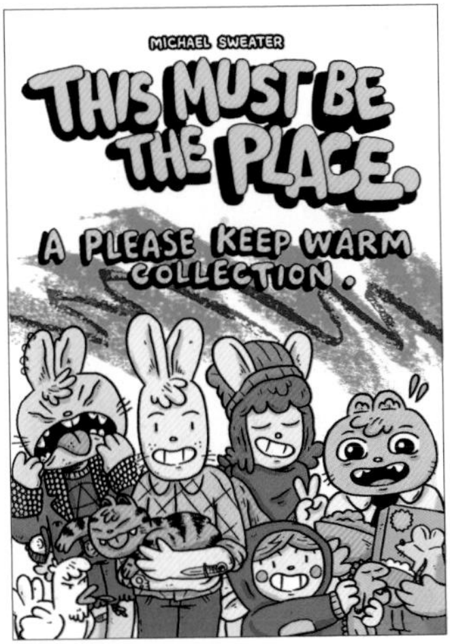
MICHAEL SWEATER
THIS MUST BE THE PLACE.
A PLEASE KEEP WARM COLLECTION.

THIS MUST BE THE PLACE, A PLEASE KEEP WARM COLLECTION.
IS A COMIC ABOUT FRIENDSHIP, OVERCOMING DEPRESSION, FINDING YOUR PLACE IN THE WORLD, AND ALSO SOMETIMES BLACK METAL.

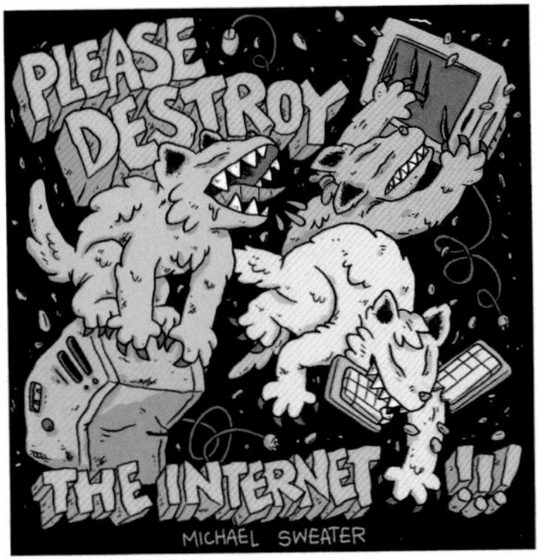
PLEASE DESTROY
THE INTERNET !!!
MICHAEL SWEATER

PLEASE DESTROY THE INTERNET IS THE FOLLOW UP TO THIS BOOK YOU ARE LOOKING AT RIGHT NOW.
FEATURING SUCH NEW CHARACTERS AS KARATE DAD, MAN WHO HATES COMPUTERS, AND THE FERAL GIRL.
THIS BOOK IS SURE TO PLEASE ANYONE WHO HATES TWITTER, THE GOVERNMENT, OR JUST THEMSELVES.

STORE.SILVERSPROCKET.NET/SWEATER